25

Beasts and Bawdy

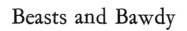

Beasts and Bawdy

Anne Clark

Taplinger Publishing Company
New York

First published in the United States in 1975 by
TAPLINGER PUBLISHING CO., INC.
New York, New York

Library of Congress Catalog Card Number: 75–807
ISBN 0-8008-0691-3

Contents

List of Illustrations

7

Acknowledgments

The author and publishers are grateful to the following for permission to quote extracts from the works cited:

Burns and Oates, *The Ancrene Riwle*, translated by M. B. Salu; Jonathan Cape Ltd, *The Georgics of Virgil*, translated by C. Day Lewis; The Clarendon Press, Oxford, *The Complete Works of John Lyly*, edited by J. Warwick Bond; The Early English Text Society and the Oxford University Press, *The Bodley Version of Mandeville's Travels*, edited by M. C. Seymour; Faber & Faber Ltd, *The Works of Sir Thomas Browne*, edited by Geoffrey Keynes; William Heinemann Ltd, *Natural History*, by Pliny, edited by H. Rackham, Loeb Classical Library, and *De natura animalium*, by Aelian, translated by A. F. Scholfield; Penguin Books Ltd, *The Canterbury Tales*.

Also to the British Library, Cambridge University Library; Corpus Christi Library, Cambridge; Metropolitan Museum of Art, New York; and Musée de Cluny, Paris, for permission to reproduce illustrations.

CHAPTER ONE
Sources of Animal Lore

ONCE UPON A TIME men thought the world was filled with monsters: with dragons and unicorns, long-haired hippopotami and weird savage men who covered their bottoms with their own long ears.

If you ventured too near the edge of the earth you had to take care, for a man might easily be turned to stone by a glance from the dreaded catoblepas, or mauled to death by the fearsome martichoras. A woman, on the other hand, might easily find herself 'filthily abused' by the satyrus ape, at whose hands she would undoubtedly meet a fate even worse than death.

Medieval lore of this kind, which our forbears took very seriously, evolved slowly, and its origins are both ancient and obscure. The animal world made a strong appeal to the imagination and offered a challenge to the artistic and creative instincts of the human race which it rose to meet from the earliest known times, as demonstrated in the cave-art of the Upper Paleolithic people. Side by side with this artistic depiction of beasts arose a powerful oral tradition whose ultimate sources must remain speculative.

In the days when books were rare and precious things owned only by the very rich, or by certain kinds of religious institutions, the influences of the oral tradition were especially strong. Our knowledge of this tradition is limited to the inferences we can draw from such books as have been handed down and from such cultural relics as have survived the passage of time. We cannot easily understand the reasons why it developed as it did. Perhaps it is partly explained by man's deep-seated need in a world that was still largely unexplored to prepare himself for any eventuality.

It cannot be denied that a great thirst for information is one of man's most basic instincts, being closely associated with the fundamental human preoccupations of survival, of finding food and clothing in adequate quantity, of general care of the body and of the procreation and nurture of children. Mankind had always to exercise his powers of invention, the retentiveness of his memory and his reasoning ability in order to maintain a footing in a world where many animals were larger, stronger and better equipped for combat than himself. In addition he had to contend with inanimate forces of nature, such as earthquakes, fire and flood, all of which were capable of robbing him of his precarious existence.

This deeply rooted desire for knowledge was the over-riding force which enabled man not only to survive but also to raise himself above the level of brute existence, and to surround himself with a reasonably acceptable social environment. The same impulse led men to find the means of conversing and, later, of writing, in order that items of the data could be exchanged with other people and circulated to contemporaries even in remote regions, as well as handed down for the enlightenment of posterity.

Under this impetus human knowledge expanded with enormous rapidity. Mankind was possessed with the fevered desire to acquire new facts. There may even have been an instinctive compulsion to fill the gaps in human knowledge at all costs, even if necessary by invention.

Certainly the early map-makers employed their imaginations liberally in this way. Henry Peacham, a seventeenth-century geographer, advised cartographers to cover their maps with naked boys riding on goats, with satyrs, tritons, and cornucopias as well as 'with a thousand more such idle toyes, so that herein you cannot be too fantastical'. Swift, writing more than a century later, satirizes this practice:

> So geographers, in Afric maps,
> With savage pictures fill their gaps,
> And o'er inhabitable downs,
> Place elephants for want of towns.

The unfettered imagination had not always played such an important role in man's efforts to acquire knowledge about the world in which he lived. In ancient Greece the attitude to learning had been remarkably responsible, and the concept of rational organization of ideas based on accurate observation had played a major part in the development of knowledge. This outlook had been passed to the Romans, but when the Roman Empire fell into a state of decay and finally crumbled in the fifth century A.D. these guiding principles were lost for many centuries. With the fall of Rome Christianity established itself as the new force which controlled the western world.

Modern scientific analysis has now almost completely ousted the old accounts of the bawdy and bewildering beasts that lived and multiplied in the naïve but fertile imaginations of our ancestors. Although even today there are gaps in what we know of the way in which animals function, we are at least broadly aware of the limitations of our own knowledge.

Yet the proper scientific observation of animal behaviour is a comparatively recent development. For much of recorded history—from ancient times until the late seventeenth century—knowledge of the animal kingdom largely consisted of a curious mixture of travellers' tales, fable and extravagant invention. In our advanced technological society we tend to forget the enormous gulf between our present-day proven knowledge of the animal kingdom and the splendidly absurd notions accepted as true facts less than three hundred years ago.

Often, however, it is possible to work out some of the reasoning processes that lay behind the old beliefs. There seems, for instance, to have been a genuine intellectual dilemma underlying the notions of the strange postures adopted by elephants during copulation. It is fairly clear that the great weight of the elephant puzzled our forbears, who obviously thought that if the male mounted the female in the manner common to quadrupeds, he would inevitably crush her. Many of the theories about the sex life of the elephant, as detailed in chapter five of this book, were there-

fore aimed at suggesting an alternative method of coition in
which the weight problem would either be overcome completely or at least minimized.

It is not difficult to see that inadequate opportunities for
observation and lack of sophisticated scientific equipment
were responsible for many mistaken beliefs about animals.
Herodotus, a historian of the fifth century B.C. who included
many items of zoological data in his works, described one
animal in the following terms:

It is a quadruped, cloven-footed, with hoofs like an ox, and
a flat nose. It has the mane and tail of a horse, huge tusks
which are very conspicuous, and a voice like a horse's neigh.
In size it equals the biggest oxen, and its skin is so tough
that when dried it is made into javelins.

Presumably Herodotus, though well travelled, had had
little or no opportunity for direct personal observation of
the animal he was writing about, and few twentieth-century
readers would identify the hippopotamus from this description.

A medieval writer nearly two thousand years later was
even more inaccurate, confusing the hippopotamus with the
fabulous hippocentaur, a composite beast, and adding that it
had a marked preference for human flesh: 'In that reume arn
a maner of bestys that aryn callid (y)potami that wonyn as
wel in the watir as on the lond, the which bestys the on half
of hem hath the shap of a man and that othir half of an hors.
They etyn men whan euere thay may getyn hem, nothing
leuere of no manere mete.' *

Nevertheless, as one might expect, people who lived in
countries where the hippopotamus was common could
produce a much more accurate picture. Present-day visitors
to the Metropolitan Museum of Art in New York can see a
tiny statue of a hippopotamus, affectionately known to New
Yorkers as William, which was made in Egypt during the
period of the Middle Kingdom, nearly four thousand years
ago. Though fancifully coloured turquoise and decorated

* In that country is a species of animal called hippopotami, which are equally at
home in water and on land. One half of these beasts is shaped like a man and the
other half resembles a horse. They devour men whenever they can catch them,
preferring them above all other kinds of meat.

with flowers, it is beautifully proportioned and instantly recognizable, possessing not a single hint of mane or tusk.

Heredotus was by no means wholly naïve in his zoological accounts, and although for example he described the phoenix, now known to be fabulous, at some length, he also included his own personal observations on the reliability of the accounts which he had received second-hand:

> They tell a story of what this bird does, which does not seem to me to be credible: that he comes all the way from Arabia, and brings the parent bird, all plastered over with myrrh, to the Temple of the Sun, and there buries the body. In order to bring him, they say, he first forms a ball of myrrh as big as he finds he can carry; then he hollows out the ball, and puts his parent inside, after which he covers the opening with fresh myrrh, and the ball is then of exactly the same weight as at first; so he brings it to Egypt, plastered over as I have said, and deposites it in the Temple of the Sun. Such is the story they tell of the doings of this bird.

During the reign of Alexander the Great the need for a responsible scientist to gather all known facts about the animal kingdom into an authoritative textbook became apparent. The man commissioned to organize and execute this gigantic undertaking was none other than Aristotle, the great philosopher and political thinker and one-time tutor to Alexander himself.

Perhaps Aristotle had inherited his scientific spirit from his father, who had been a famous court physician. His prime interest lay in the classification of the various species, and in the world of organic nature. Once he wrote: 'The more I find myself by myself and alone, the more I become a lover of myth.' Yet, with few exceptions, myth and fable are notably absent from his biological analyses.

The result of Aristotle's research was a book written in the fourth century B.C. which he entitled *Historia Animalium* (History of Animals), and which was by far the best zoological work produced in classical times. It was drawn up in a systematic and highly scientific fashion, and was based on much personal observation supplemented by the discriminating use of other responsible authorities. Data obtained during Alexander's own expeditions were apparently made freely available for inclusion in the survey.

Though he was acknowledged to be a master philosopher in the Middle Ages, Aristotle's biological and other scientific work had to wait until the twentieth century before its merit was fully realized. By a curious anomaly his zoological writings were neglected in favour of the more popular works of his later rivals, who drew freely on his books but were less well able to distinguish between fact and fable.

Most popular of all these rivals was Pliny the Elder, whose *Natural History*, in thirty-seven volumes, included four volumes on zoology and a further four on animal medicines. This was regarded as a major textbook even as late as the seventeenth century, and is noted as such in Milton's *Tractate on Education*. His nephew, Pliny the Younger, describes him as a dedicated scholar who, having daily paid his respects to the Roman Emperor Vespasian, devoted the remainder of his time to scholarly pursuits.

It was Pliny's custom to take copious notes from everything that he read, for according to his philosophy no book could be so inept that it contained nothing of value. Even in the bath he could not afford to waste a moment, but listened to readings from learned texts while relaxing in the water, or dictated to a secretary while being rubbed down.

Pliny the Elder was about fifty-five years old when he lost his life in the eruption of Vesuvius in A.D. 79. According to his nephew, he sailed from Misenum, where he was stationed as prefect of the Roman fleet, to Castellamare in order to be with those who were in danger. Here he dined cheerfully doing everything that he could to restore the spirits of his friends before eventually being overcome by fumes in the general exodus to the seashore.

Though Pliny wrote various other books, his *Natural History* is the only one which has survived. In this he draws freely on other writers, and is heavily indebted to Aristotle. He was, however, far less discriminating in his use of other sources, tending to accept statements from almost any writer as equally valid. His organization of material was less scientific than Aristotle's, his normal method being to start with the largest and work down. Thus elephants begin the book on land animals, whales and sharks the book on marine life, while ostriches take precedence in the book on birds.

Other classical authors who should be mentioned are Ctesias, the Greek of the fourth century B.C., who had travelled extensively abroad and was personal physician to the king of Persia; Theophrastus, a successor to Aristotle of the third century B.C., who exhibited something of the same scientific spirit; Solinus, who lived a century later than Pliny and did little more than copy his works, concentrating on the more sensational and less responsible aspects of them; and Aelian in the third century, a loquacious and haphazard Roman author who ignored the work of his own countrymen and wrote his books in Attic Greek, quoting Greek writers as his only authorities.

The Bible in its Hebrew version and its various translated forms as well as the commentaries on them were major influences on our ancestors' concept of animal lore up to the middle of the seventeenth century. By the end of the third century B.C. a large colony of Jews had settled permanently in Alexandria. Gradually over the course of several generations they had lost the Hebrew tongue, and without it proper attention to the teaching of the Bible had become virtually impossible. It was therefore decided that the Old Testament would have to be translated for their benefit from the original Hebrew into Greek. With this object in mind a huge team of translators was specially selected in Jerusalem and sent to Alexandria, where the mammoth task was undertaken.

The work of these scholars made the Hebrew Bible, with its numerous references to animals, available for the first time throughout the Greek sphere of influence. Their version was known as the *Septuagint*, the name being taken from the number of translators, though there were apparently seventy-two of these, and not seventy, as the name suggests.

Errors of translation crept into the Septuagint from time to time, sometimes because the beasts described in the original pages were the outcome of inadequate observation, primitive superstition and myth. This posed difficult problems for the translators, but even more formidable obstacles were the rather restricted biological terminology of the day and the inadequate differentiation between the various species in the Hebrew language, where the same word often had to serve for two or even more animals.

Jewish and Christian commentators alike considered themselves under an obligation to provide an adequate explanation for those things in the Septuagint which puzzled them, and allowed their fertile imaginations to supply the answers when their store of knowledge failed. When the Septuagint was translated at a later date into Latin, and revised in a version known as the Vulgate, some of the original errors were perpetuated and new ones were added. This gave rise to a whole series of further commentaries, so that the pattern was repeated.

Among the most important moralizing accounts of animals which circulated widely in the early Christian era were the *Homilies of Origen* (A.D. 186–253), and the theological treatises about the creation, which went under the title *The Hexameron*, and which were written by Basil (A.D. 329–379), Ambrose (A.D. 340–397) and Eusthathius (fl. *c.* A.D. 450).

In the seventh century an important new ecclesiastical writer came upon the scene whose writings were to have wide implications for the future shaping of beast lore: Isidore of Seville. Isidore was an orphan who was placed in a monastery to be educated at an early age, dedicated himself to a life of religion and ultimately became a bishop.

In the view of Isidore, education was absolutely essential to the work of the evangelist and the man of God. So strong was his conviction that vice was encouraged by ignorance that he instituted a school for intending priests and a library in Seville concerning which little has been handed down to us. We do know, however, that he personally supervised the training of clerics in the compilation of material, and that silence and strictly correct behaviour were absolute rules, so that a man might even have to submit to corporal punishment for failing to observe silence in the scriptorium or wasting time by day-dreaming. Idlers and chatterers were ruthlessly dismissed from this form of religious service.

An insatiable reader himself, Isidore saw no reason to omit profane literature from the onerous course of studies which he pursued. His vast knowledge in many branches of learning enabled him to transmit information to others in a huge output of encyclopaedias and books which he wrote on such subjects as ethics, theology, history, etc.

As a historian and encyclopaedic writer Isidore was haphazard and uncritical, but his books were popular and helped to convey remnants of classical scholarship to Europe. His greatest love was grammar, with heavy emphasis on the origin of words, but his most popular work, the *Etymology*, was left in an unfinished state at his death in 636, and had to be corrected subsequently by his friend Braulio, Bishop of Saragossa.

Isidore's works were famous during his lifetime and immediately after his death. They were transmitted to future generations in the fascinating beast-books or bestiaries of the Middle Ages, which are described in full in chapter two of this book. Later the ideas of Isidore and the bestiarists were incorporated into various encyclopaedic works which had now become fashionable.

A twelfth-century abbot called Alexander Neckam, whose mother had been wet-nurse to King Richard I, with whom he had been brought up, wrote an important encyclopaedical treatise called *De naturis rerum* ('About the things of Nature'). Neckam was a distinguished lecturer who had achieved fame in Paris as well as popularity in English court circles, and his work, written in about the year 1180, was highly regarded both in England and on the Continent.

During the following century Bartholomew Anglicus, the Englishman, sometimes erroneously referred to as Bartholomew Glanvil, leapt to fame with his book *De Proprietatibus Rerum* ('On the Properties of Things'), a medieval encyclopaedia in nineteen volumes. The facts contained in his work were so arranged as to focus attention sharply on certain religious and moral values. Because of its immense

popular appeal the work was translated into English by
Trevisa in the fourteenth century, and printed in 1495 by
Wynkyn de Worde, the poor continental apprentice who
became a master printer and eventually took over Caxton's
printing works.

By the late sixteenth century three freely abridged and
augmented versions of Trevisa's translation had appeared.
The last and most popular of these was by a doctor of
divinity called Stephen Batman. His version appeared in
1582 under the pretentious title *Batman uppon Bartholome, His
Booke De Proprietatibus Rerum; newly corrected, enlarged and
amended, with such Additions as are required, unto every severall
Booke*. It was, he explains, 'Taken forth of the most approved Authors the like heretofore not translated, in
English'. According to Batman, this book would prove
'Profitable for all Estates, as well for the benefit of the Mind
as the Bodie'.

From the thirteenth century onwards, European and
world travellers' tales gained an ever-increasing vogue, and
stories of the exploits of adventurers like Marco Polo, a
medieval commercial traveller who found favour at the
court of Kublai Khan, Odoric, the Franciscan friar who
travelled extensively in Asia as a missionary, and others
helped to strengthen and increase the wealth of animal lore
already in circulation.

Not all travellers' tales of this kind were genuine. A
mystery writer who hid his true identity under the pseu-
donym 'Sir John Mandeville' baffled not only men of his
own generation but scholars of each succeeding century.
According to his deathbed confession the true author was a
bearded Liége physician called Jehan de Bourgogne. Who-
ever the real writer was, he had a powerful imagination and
borrowed quite shamelessly from genuine travellers, and the
extent of these borrowings calls into question the authen-
ticity of the whole book, which he entitled *The Voyage of
Sir John Mandeville*.

As the new sea routes to the East and West Indies were
opened up, the growing spirit of adventure, added to the
potential advantages of improved commerce, provided

powerful incentives for foreign travel. Those returning from voyages overseas were now able either to corroborate the old beliefs about animals, or alternatively to correct the mistaken ideas of the past. Their silence on certain topics was in time almost equally revealing. It became clear that many beasts formerly accepted as part of the animal kingdom were nowhere to be found, and people accordingly began seriously to call into question the existence of such beasts.

Men now began to collect biological specimens which helped to supplement, substantiate or disprove existing data. Some of this material was actually put on display to the English public for the first time. Museums were by no means a new idea, for the first can be traced back to Athens of the second century A.D., but the idea seems to have been dropped and reintroduced very slowly and only after many hundreds of years had elapsed. Perhaps it was encouraged by the displays of religious reliques in the Middle Ages, and from the prestigious collections which wealthy men exhibited privately to their friends in the Renaissance period. The *cabinet de curiosités* kept by Francis I at Fontainebleau was one example, and the famous collection of Ole Worm, the Danish physician, was another.

But it was not until the seventeenth century that John Tradescant and his son of the same name introduced the first museum or 'arch of novelties' to England. Both father and son, who were successively head court gardeners, had travelled widely abroad, and as serious botanists and zoologists had brought back many specimens which they later placed on exhibition and which ultimately became the basis of the famous Ashmole Museum in Oxford.

Nevertheless these so-called specimens could often be misleading, even to serious biologists. Tradescant's museum catalogue for the year 1656 listed 'Two feathers of the Phoenix tayle', and 'A natural dragon above two inches long'. Deliberate fraud, often for financial profit on an outrageous scale, was often practised, as for example in the case of 'unicorn' horns, so highly prized that even in the seventeenth century the horns of other animals were often offered for sale in their stead. Deceptions of this kind also helped to encourage the spread of false information.

In the year 1551 a versatile Swiss medical practitioner and lecturer in physics called Konrad von Gesner brought out the first of a five-volume series of zoological textbooks entitled *Historia Animalium*, a gigantic, impressive piece of work which even today is looked on by some people as the beginning of modern zoology. Gesner's work was introduced to the English public in 1607 by Edward Topsell, in *The Historie of foure-footed Beastes* and, a year later, in *The Historie of Serpents*. Although Topsell regarded himself as a serious contributor to the cause of zoological research, his books are rich in popular misconceptions and naïvely illustrated with fanciful drawings, some of them taken from Gesner. His title-page is shown in Plate 5.

Finally all these sources have to be looked at in the light of the works of John Lyly, elegant prose-writer, poet and dramatist of the Elizabethan era, who leapt to fame virtually overnight with the publication in the year 1578 of his first book, *Euphues, or The Anatomy of Wit*.

While others were travelling throughout the world in search of adventure and new discoveries, Lyly explored the uses of language. Unashamedly he admitted that his principal aim was to amuse ladies in their drawing-rooms rather than to instruct scholars. To this end he employed antithesis and alliteration, and made use of nicely balanced sentence structure to produce a highly complicated, ornate style. Elaborate conceits and frequent references to animals were a feature of Lyly's style, as in the following passage where he argues that infants should be breast-fed by their own mothers, and not put out to a wet nurse:

It is most necessary and most naturall in mine opinion, that the mother of the childe be also the nurse, both for the entire love she beareth to the babe, and the great desire she hath to have it well nourished: . . . Whatsoever is bred in ye sea is fed in the sea; no plant, no tree, no hearbe commeth out of the ground that is not moystened, and as it were noursed of the moysture and mylke of the earth; the lyonesse nurseth hir whelps, the raven cherisheth hir byrdes, the viper her broode, and shal a woman cast away her babe? . . . and can it be tearmed with any other title then cruelty, the infant yet looking redde of the mother, the mother yet breathing through the torments of hir travaile, the child crying for helpe which is said to move wilde beastes, even in the selfe said moment it is borne, or the nexte minute, to deliver to a strange nurse, which perhappes is neither wholesome in body, neither honest in manners, which esteemeth more thy tender infant, thy greatest treasure?

The beasts which he describes are often endowed with traits of human psychology, and there are innumerable references to their physical attributes and imputed psychological characteristics. Where it suited his literary purposes, Lyly had no qualms about supplementing the data assembled by the bestiarists and classical writers, but included his own extravagant pieces of zoological fantasy as an addition to other items.

So popular did Lyly's writings become that many of his contemporaries, like Nashe, Gosson and Greene, imitated his manner of writing. Not content with this, people also began to imitate him in their speech patterns, and Charles Blount, his first editor, claimed that 'that Beautie in Court, which could not Parley Euphuism, was as little regarded; as shee which now there, speakes not French'.

Such an artificial style, though interesting, could not remain popular for long. After a vogue of little more than a decade the fashion for this 'Euphuistic' manner began to fall into a rapid decline. By the time that Shakespeare came to write *King Henry IV*, Part 1, we find him including a parody of this style of writing:

For though the camomile, the more it is trodden on the faster it grows, yet youth, the more it is wasted the sooner it wears. . . . There is a thing, Harry, which thou hast often heard of, and it is known to many in our land by the name of pitch: this pitch, as ancient writers do report, doth defile; so doth the company thou keepest; for, Harry, now I do not speak to thee in drink, but in tears, not in pleasure but in passion, not in words only, but in woes also.

As a result of the great advances in zoological knowledge which have taken place in the last three centuries we have forgotten the old fables which were once accepted as solid fact. The many references to animals in the works of Shakespeare and his contemporaries have therefore become largely unintelligible to the present-day reader. An attempt to understand the background of animal lore in medieval, Elizabethan and Jacobean times can be richly rewarding both for the sake of its intrinsic interest and because it increases our enjoyment of the drama, poetry and prose writings of these critical phases in the development of English literature, and helps us to gain some insight into the minds of Shakespeare and his contemporaries.

By the time Shakespeare embarked on his career as a writer he had already outgrown Lyly's prose style but, country boy though he was, his animal lore was often no more scientific. Man's grasp of nature was still a glorious, though codified, jumble of fact, fable and invention when Shakespeare left his native Warwickshire and came to London. As a full-time professional actor and dramatist, he made good use of animal lore, and particularly of the medieval bestiaries, which are explained in the next chapter. Whether he had direct knowledge of the bestiaries is open to conjecture; but their teaching had certainly been handed down in the literature of Elizabethan England.

CHAPTER TWO

Physiologus *and the* Bestiaries

'THE HEDGEHOG has a kind of prudence for when the grapes fall from the vine, it rolls upside down on the bunch, and so brings it back to its young.'

'The hyena has a stone in its eye, called a yena, which is said to make a man see into the future, if he keeps it under his tongue. If a hyena walks three times round any animal, he paralyses it.'

'When a monkey gives birth to twins, she loves one and hates the other. If chased by a hunter, she clasps the one she loves in her arms, and takes the one she hates on her back. When she is exhausted by running on her hind legs, she lets fall the one she loves, while the one she hates still clings to her shoulders.'

These are typical examples of the naïve kind of animal lore offered by the bestiarists for the enlightenment of mankind.

What exactly are the bestiaries, and how did they originate? Present-day readers, intrigued by the quaint and often unashamedly bawdy text, might be forgiven for supposing that they were produced by some kind of medieval pornographer. This would be a wholly false assumption, for they were in fact the work of the monasteries, copied out by pious men for their own moral profit, as well as for the enlightenment of their fellows.

The story of the female elephant offering the mandrake root to her mate to induce him to copulate must therefore be looked on not as false data but as an essential reminder of Adam and Eve and the apple, while the tale of the beaver castrating himself in the presence of the hunter is not just a

salacious story but an indication—not to be taken too
literally—of man's obligation to cast from him the lusts and
sins of the flesh.

The moral which concludes the chapter on the antelope is
typical of the teaching of the bestiaries. The antelope,
according to the accounts, loves to play with the herecine
tree, found on the banks of the Euphrates. But having
entwined its antlers in the long branches, it is unable to get
free, and the hunter, hearing its loud bellows, comes along
and kills it.

Go and do thou likewise, O man of God, seeking a pure
spiritual life! The two testaments are your anthers, to cut
off the sins of the flesh, adultery, fornication, greed, envy,
pride, murder, gossip, intemperance, lust and worldly
display. Angels will bestow on you the rewards of heaven.
But avoid the tree of inebriety, and do not become ensnared
by carnal pleasure, or you may be slain by the devil. Wine
and women easily seduce men from God.

A bestiary is in reality a moral and religious treatise in
which the supposed characteristics of animals are used to
illustrate points of doctrinal and moral significance. Perhaps
the popularity of the animal fable had helped to bring this
genre into being; but in fables, single animals had been
endowed with qualities normally associated with human
beings in order to provide a moral lesson, usually on a
rather elementary ethical plane, while in the bestiaries the
characteristics of a whole species are used for religious or
ethical didacticism.

The direct source of the bestiaries was an anonymous
book called *Physiologus* or 'The Naturalist'. Over the centuries there was much speculation about the identity of the
writer, and King Solomon and Aristotle are among the many
who have been credited with this work, but the real author
has never been discovered.

As to the original manuscript, this has not survived, but
it is thought to have been written at some time between the
second and fourth centuries A.D. in Alexandria, the city
where the Septuagint version of the Old Testament was
produced. Many of the ideas in the bestiaries can be directly

traced to the large body of Jewish and Christian commentary generated by the Septuagint and the various later translations of the Bible.

By a careful analysis of later manuscripts drawn from various sources, modern scholars have been able to construct a list of forty-nine animal chapters, usually identifiable by their greater crudity, which almost without doubt made up the first text, and these animals were all known to the Alexandrian of the period, either through direct experience or from available literature. As to the illustrations, these were thought to be in the contemporary Alexandrian style, and to have provided the authority for future copies.

The religious creeds which confronted the Alexandrian Greek at that time—Egyptian, Jewish, Syriac, Persian and Roman—all asserted that the world was ruled by a powerful force of evil which could only be overcome by religion. Perhaps the author of *Physiologus* felt that by translating moral values into the sort of symbolic terms which provided a link with the universal use of mystic ritual and formula he could undermine the domination of evil.

In their intense preoccupation with the occult meaning of words, the early Christian Fathers, who strongly favoured the symbolic method of teaching, ransacked the various translations of the Bible in their search for hidden meanings, and felt under an unavoidable obligation to explain anything they found there whose meaning was in any way obscure.

Its heavy emphasis on symbolism and moral didacticism indicates that *Physiologus* was meant not so much as a zoological handbook but as a religious treatise. At some periods in its history the Christian Church, fearing its potential undermining of religious dogma, treated scientific discovery with some hostility. Because they were conceived in a basically heathen society the works of Greek and Roman scholars of the past were ignored. It was thought that an important function of the animal kingdom was to act as an example to mankind, and instead of searching for the scientific truth about beast behaviour men were expected to seek out the moral values which God was believed to have hidden there.

But whether the Church approved or not, it was in the event impossible to blot out the beliefs which had dominated the human imagination for so many centuries. Though the *Historia Animalium* of Aristotle, which was the best zoological manual available until the sixteenth century, was largely ignored, the popular ideas of such writers as Pliny the Elder, Aelian and Solinus still held strong.

The author of *Physiologus* was not a genuine naturalist. He could not offer any first-hand scientific observation to support his theories, and made no real contribution to our knowledge of the way in which the animal kingdom behaves. His teaching was primarily concerned with moral and doctrinal interpretation, and when it came to biological data he had to rely on the work of earlier authors, even though these were mostly heathen.

Physiologus was so popular that before long it had been translated into many other tongues, beginning, it is believed, with Ethiopian, Armenian, Syriac and Arabic, and followed by Latin and the Romance languages. Manuscripts in all these have survived, as well as Persian, Anglo-Saxon, Old High German and Icelandic. As to Greek versions, these are represented only by comparatively late examples, the oldest dating only from the eleventh century.

At a synod held in A.D. 496, and believed to have been presided over by Pope Gelasius, *Physiologus* was banned. Yet even being proscribed in this way did little to reduce its popularity.

During the eleventh century cathedral cities, and notably those at Chartres and Orleans, began to set new standards of learning. Now, instead of remaining in isolated rural monasteries, the best scholars of the age flocked together to exchange ideas and impart knowledge.

At this period the major Greek writers of the past were chiefly known through those Latin texts which had managed to survive the Dark Ages in western Europe. Boethius was regarded particularly highly, and he had handed down the works of Plato and Aristotle. But he had been principally interested in their achievement in ethics and logic, and had ignored their scientific works. The scientific works of

Aristotle were received at third or fourth hand from Pliny and his later imitators through the abstracts of Isidore of Seville. As interest in zoology increased, scholars realized that another book was available which dealt exclusively with animals: *Physiologus*.

The text of *Physiologus* had never been regarded as static. Whenever it had suited the changing needs of the times it had been amended. Old-fashioned ideas had been dropped, and new data had been added as the book had circulated from country to country and from one language group to another.

Now the bestiarists of the Middle Ages took over *Physiologus*. They re-examined it critically, and having assessed the special needs of their own era adapted their techniques and began to develop and expand it. Besides adding extra data to existing entries, they included many more animals, and prefaced almost every beast chapter with a fanciful etymology based on the work of Isidore.

The bestiaries passed through four main stages of development and expansion.

Stage one saw the best descriptions from *Physiologus* supplemented by data drawn from Isidore. Except for the fanciful etymologies which were included this was based on fairly accurate zoological fact.

Stage two, which dates from the twelfth century, was a period of extensive revision to the whole work, both illustrative and textual. An important feature was the re-arrangement of chapters into a logical sequence of beasts, birds, fish and reptiles. New material was drawn not only from Isidore but also from Solinus, and from contemporary writers like Giraldus Cambrensis and Hugo de Folieto. The number of animals included in most texts in this group was at least twice as many as in the original *Physiologus*.

The third stage partially overlaps the second, and is composed of a small group which seems to have been recast independently of the rest in the thirteenth century. An important innovation is the inclusion of chapters on the fabulous notions and seven wonders of the world, drawn from Isidore and Bernard Silvestris. In addition there are

medical remedies from Seneca and divinations from John
of Salisbury.

A single fifteenth-century bestiary with additions taken
from Isidore and from Bartholomew Anglicus forms stage
four.

The task of the bestiary illustrators was to emphasize the
animal characteristics defined in the text, and as long as the
pictures conformed with a convention which the reader
could recognize and identify with the doctrinal and moral
principles indicated by the text the crudest of drawings
would have served. Although the hotch-potch of Christian
symbolism, scientific observation and folklore invited
imaginative graphic invention, the illustrators were not free
to portray their subjects realistically, being bound strictly
by the religious slant of the theologians.

Two important bestiaries are known which are illustrated
in an early Alexandrian style possibly based on the original
Physiologus manuscript. Both contain traces of naturalism,
but the attempt at naturalistic portrayal seems to have died
out by the tenth century. Similarly, illustrations of Christian
homily following the description of the beast were sometimes found in early copies. Christ, the devil, etc., were
featured in such illustrations, but by the twelfth century
these were usually omitted altogether except in pictures of
the Creation and Naming of the Animals, which at that
period would have been regarded as zoology. An obvious
inference is that at this point in time the bestiaries had come
to be valued more for their zoology than for their theology.

Side by side with the revitalizing of the text came the
revision of the illustrations. This was really a continuation
of the Latin revival of learning, for instead of relying on
direct personal observation of nature, the illustrators turned
to time-honoured tradition, not only in respect of such
animals as whales and crocodiles, which the artist might
never have seen with his own eyes, but for foxes, dogs,
horses, etc., which were a familiar part of daily life.

But now that the bestiaries had expanded the medieval
illustrator was faced with a difficulty. Writers who enlarged
the text could go to the work of well-loved authorities like

Isidore, but for the artist there was no equivalent authoritative source. Most would have found it beyond their ability to take nature as a model, and instead of trusting to their own judgment they ransacked ancient traditional sources.

Sometimes the old fable illustrations served this purpose, but so great was the expansion of the bestiaries that fables alone could not provide sufficient examples. Eventually men solved the problem by taking over and adapting heraldic depictions of beasts passed on in the industrial arts of the Middle East.

This meant that the shapeless drawings of the past were replaced by disciplined designs, often cunningly set in squares and roundels. The elongated human form of native tradition was still preferred, and sometimes as a result the picture is cramped, but the best illustrators adapted their styles to the new designs with great success, often using fine colours, and isolating the animals against a splendid gold background.

By the late thirteenth century the bestiary animals had cast off their imprisoning roundels and now, decked in trailing leaves, gambolled unrestrained in the margins, as in Plate 12.

Physiologus had known popularity, but the bestiaries stimulated an enthusiasm which ranked them with the Psalter and the Apocalypse. Their designs infiltrated other artistic spheres, and the beasts in their characteristic postures are to be found in paintings and mosaics, in tapestry and cloth. They also invaded church architecture on a wide scale and are still to be found carved in wood or stone on choir stalls and joints or above doorways and on columns, where their presence served to remind the faithful of their moral duty. While bestiaries could influence contemporary thinking on this scale, it is small wonder that men of religion worked assiduously to produce more and more copies.

What were they like, the men who prepared the bestiary manuscripts so many centuries ago, and how did they carry out their work?

Many of them would have been monks, but not all, for as the demand for books increased it became the practice to employ secular scribes in order to maintain the high output required. In most religious orders daily private reading of sacred books was obligatory, and this meant that a relatively high standard of education was required, both in order that the books could be read and also to enable them to be produced.

Though many were secular scribes living outside the monastery walls almost all of them were educated in the monasteries, for it was here that the great medieval schools were principally set up. Many of the boys who were sent to the monastic schools were intended from a very early age to become monks, but others were admitted who were not destined for the monastic life. Wherever the accommodation and teaching facilities permitted, however, the lay brothers received separate courses of education from the secular pupils.

A manuscript dating from the early eighth century entitled *Joca Monachorum*, or *Monks' Jokes*, indicates that not all the preoccupations of the holy brothers were serious ones. It includes such strange and bawdy riddles as the following:

Who knew her son before her husband? Mary, who knew Christ.

Who was born of his sister, and raped his virgin grandmother? Adam, who was born of the earth and sowed seed on it. *

Manuscript production was regarded as an important function of the monastery, and a special place was set aside for it, called the scriptorium, or workshop. The concept of workshops for book production was not a new one, for they had existed for the writing and illustration of manuscripts in Egypt, where they flourished on a wide scale in the period of the Middle Kingdom, that is, between the twenty-first and eighteenth centuries B.C.

One of the finest illuminated bestiary manuscripts in existence, which was rescued from a German bookseller by the poet William Morris and is now in the Pierpont Morgan Library, New York, was presented to the Augustinian Priory of Radford (now Worksop), Nottinghamshire, in A.D. 1187 by Philip, Canon of Lincoln. It became the custom

* Quoted from Jean Decarreaux: *Monks and Civilization*, Allen & Unwin, 1964.

for royalty and the rich to commission books specially from the monasteries, so that the output of codices was no longer reserved for the cloister alone.

Book production was not the only industry carried on in the scriptorium during the Middle Ages. As a natural development from the primary function, deeds, wills, letters, etc., were prepared under the direction of the principal scribe. Any work carried out for outsiders was a valuable additional source of revenue for the monasteries.

The chief scribe also acted as head librarian, being responsible for purchasing books or borrowing them from other monasteries for copying. Because books were costly and rare, they were stacked in chests in a separate library, which had to be kept permanently locked. At the time when the Radford Priory bestiary was produced, a library of some three hundred books would have been considered quite a large one.

Papyrus imported from Egypt was the writing material usually employed until the beginning of the eighth century. It was made from the pith of a reed related to the bulrush, which grew in abundance in the Nile Delta. The method of producing it was to cut the pith into fine strips and to join them horizontally, adding to this another layer joined in the opposite direction and glued to the first layer. When glazed and dried, the sheets were formed into rolls which would be inscribed on one side only. Not more than twenty sheets usually made up a roll, and the best quality sheet, usually made from the centre of the pith, was placed on the outside, not in order to deceive the purchaser as to the quality of the roll but because, being more durable, it would protect the frailer sheets inside.

Herodotus, Theophrastus and Pliny are among the writers who have given an account of this plant and the many uses to which it could be put. According to Theophrastus, it had a tapering stem about four cubits high. The heads were fit for nothing but adorning the shrines of the gods, but the roots of these plants were good for fuel, and from the stems boats, sails, cloth and ropes as well as papyrus could be made.

By the year A.D. 800 parchment was preferred to papyrus in western Europe. This was partly because Egypt had a monopoly on papyrus, which was consequently very expensive, and also because it was not well suited to our damp climate. Parchment, on the other hand, being made from the skins of such farmyard animals as sheep and goats, and vellum, made in the same way from the skins of calves and still-born animals, could be produced locally if desired.

The method employed for producing vellum or parchment was to soak the skin in chalky water for several days. The skin was then stretched on a frame, stripped of hair and smoothed with pumice stone before being ironed and trimmed to the appropriate size. Other great advantages of parchment and vellum were that they could be inscribed on both sides, and were therefore better suited to book form, and also that if copying work was too poor or no longer needed, these materials could be washed clean and used again for something else.

Contemporary pictures of scribes at work show that they sometimes sat on a stool and rested their work on their knees, and sometimes sat at a table to write or draw. Often there was a footstool and, close at hand, perhaps on a low table, would be the codex which they had to copy. In addition there would be quills, usually from geese, swans or crows, and a little knife with which they could be sharpened. Other basic necessities would be an ink-well, and a compass to measure the spaces between the lines. Sometimes a fine needle or 'prykker' would be needed, so that the scribe could prick out the margins of several pages at once, in order to speed up the copying process.

The principal scribe was responsible for organizing the work. Sometimes a single scribe would complete an entire book, but more often it would be divided up and allocated to several men. Each man was given the appropriate number of pieces of parchment or vellum, plus the number of sheets from which he had to copy.

It was usual to work in multiples of four sheets which, folded once, would produce sixteen sides. The method of dividing up the work among several men created a problem which survived in early printing practice also, for it was essential that each man should fit the work allocated to him into the given number of pages. Just as Jacobean compositors who had spaced their work too widely at the beginning often had to squeeze up their typesetting at the end, missing out stage directions or converting lines of verse into prose for the sake of economy, so the medieval scribe who had written large at the start would often have to cramp his letters at the end.

Usually the scribes were responsible for trimming their own sheets of paper. A conscientious workman was very careful about matching his sheets, for that side of the parchment which had been covered with animal hairs would inevitably be slightly different in colour from the side which had been next to the flesh. By careful arrangement it was possible to place together the hair sides and the flesh sides, so that the difference was not noticeable.

Absolute silence had to be observed by the men in the scriptorium. The work took a long time and called not only for skill but also for patience. A specially important book might easily take several years to complete, though a few months was the average length of time needed. When the monks worked long hours in uncomfortable conditions they sometimes wrote notes of complaint in the margins, or exchanged notes with one another when the eye of the chief scribe was directed elsewhere.

The normal practice with regard to medieval manuscripts, including the bestiaries where it was customary to provide at least one illustration for each animal, was for the scribe to produce the written text only, leaving spaces so that a limner or illuminator could come along afterwards and draw or paint the appropriate picture. By definition, illumination meant illustrating in gold, or more rarely in silver, together with other brilliant colours. Miniatures strictly meant pictures in which the colour red predominated, and the word was derived from the Latin *minium*, meaning red paint. It was only much later that the word became restricted to mean a small portrait.

Some of the bestiary manuscripts, as for example the

'William Morris' bestiary in the Pierpont Morgan Library, New York, are illuminated in the true sense of the word, having ornate gold backgrounds which have the effect of co-ordinating the various elements in the composition. Others contain miniatures in the strict sense, as does the charming manuscript Harley 3244 in the British Museum (Plate 18). In some manuscripts spaces were left which were, in fact, never filled, and sometimes codices which began in colour were later reduced to black and white, as in the Cambridge University manuscript L1. 4.26. T. H. White puts forward the theory in respect of this manuscript that, being produced in the Cistercian monastery at Revesby, where austerity was a strict rule, the scribe and limner were affected by a regulation forbidding ornate illumination. Pictures were, however, considered an important part of the bestiaries, which were intended to be biologically instructive, and a compromise was therefore reached by retaining the pictures but dispensing with colour.

Demand for bestiaries very soon outstripped the supply, and in order to cope with this increasing market, it became the custom for one man to dictate the text to several assembled scribes. Because silence was rigidly enforced in the scriptorium, dictation usually took place in a separate room. As a result we are often able to trace associated manuscripts which were 'mass produced' in this way. For instance, there exists in the British Museum a twin (*The Royal Bestiary*) of the 'William Morris' bestiary in the Pierpont Morgan Library, whilst another is a companion-piece to a copy held in the Bodleian Library at Oxford.

In a book entitled *An English Thirteenth Century Bestiary*, Samuel A. Ives and Hellmut Lehmann-Haupt describe an important manuscript believed to be a scribes' model book. This was a major discovery which shed a light on the way in which the production of these codices could be both speeded up and standardized.

Such a model would have been invaluable in an age when Gothic art was beginning to sweep away the old conceptions, making patterns of the new styles which had to be observed a virtual necessity.

A number of medieval model books of various kinds have been identified. One of the most interesting is a fourteenth-century codex which once belonged to Samuel Pepys. This was entitled *Monks Draw: Book* and is now in Magdalene College, Cambridge. It contains fascinating sketches, including some particularly fine portraits of birds.

The bestiary model book contains a section of fourteen pages devoted to miniatures, each with a little title explaining the picture. This was followed by the text, with spaces left for the relevant illustrations, each bearing the title corresponding to the specimen picture.

Each illustration is outlined with fine pinpricks, and a larger pinprick, with which the model could be anchored to the sheet below, is to be found in the centre of the picture.

The method seems to correspond to the pouncing once used in fresco work. Here large designs were produced in a cartoon outlined with pinpricks which would be attached to the wall and rubbed over with a bag of powdered charcoal. When the cartoon was removed, the outline would remain.

The *Bestiare d'Amour*, produced in the thirteenth century by Richard de Fournival is an interesting variant of the religious bestiary. A clerk whose father had been court physician to Philippe-Auguste of France, de Fournival combined the concepts of courtly love and the scholarly allegory of the five senses with the bestiary stories. Although the illustrations follow the same model as the religious bestiaries, all moral and religious significance has been removed. Instead the *Bestiare d'Amour* takes the form of an impassioned plea by the lover to his lady, and proved fashionable in its own day.

During the late Middle Ages the Bestiaries declined in popularity and were eventually abandoned. Though they survived into the age of printing, they were represented only by a single edition, which was published in Italy during the sixteenth century. This was the *Libellus de natura animalium*, printed by Vincento Berruerio de Piedmont. By this time the scientific data were outmoded, and the bestiaries had gone full circle, being regarded for their religious teaching alone.

CHAPTER THREE

Fabulous Beasts

THE NOTION that the male lion could copulate with the female ant is, of course, utterly preposterous. Yet in the Dark Ages men really did believe that this could happen. The offspring of this incongruous union was the ant-lion, a composite beast which looked like a lion in front and an ant at the rear.

The origin of belief in this animal is almost as absurd as its notional conception. It begins with a translator of the Septuagint, one of the team of seventy-two men sent out from Jerusalem to Alexandria to produce a Greek version of the original Hebrew Bible, coming upon the word *layish*, an unusual Hebrew word meaning 'lion', used in the Book of Job. To our translator this uncommon form seemed to demand an equally out-of-the-ordinary Greek word and, casting about in his mind for a suitable Greek equivalent, he eventually decided on the word *myrmecoleon*. This rare compound was derived from the word *myrmex*, the name of a lion-like animal said to inhabit the coastal regions of Arabia. It could, however, equally well be rendered 'ant-lion', and it is here that the confusion began to creep in.

The commentators of the Septuagint were frankly puzzled by the word, having absolutely no inkling of its philological background. Yet they were unable to shirk the responsibility of producing an explanation of this beast, which God had undoubtedly created with the specific object of providing for mankind a moral lesson. When knowledge failed, fantasy came to the rescue, and it was therefore the early Christian Fathers with their fertile imaginations instead of the curiously incompatible parents who laboured and gave birth to the ant-lion.

The enormous disparity in the size of these two beasts does not seem to have troubled our forbears. It was not, after all, their function to question the Holy doctrines. Their duty was quite clearly to examine the moral significance of the story and to praise God for having found yet another way of instructing mankind through the marvellous world of nature. In any event the search for scientific knowledge would have seemed curiously irrelevant in a world where the Kingdom of God and the Day of Judgement were expected to arrive at any time.

The ant-lion could not, of course, survive for more than a few days, for it was readily apparent to our ancestors that it was unable to obtain nourishment. Since its front half resembled its father, the lion, it was by instinct a flesh-eater. Yet its carnivorous tastes if indulged would only have caused it to throw up, for its stomach, being that of an ant, could not digest meat. The lion-like front end had, however, no instinct to eat grass, the only type of food which would have proved suitable to the ant-like digestion, so that within a very short space of time the poor beast simply starved to death. As far as is known, the female lion, though much addicted to sex, never felt the urge to copulate with the male ant.

The phoenix, like the ant-lion, found its way into the Bible on account of a mistranslation. One instance of this is found in Psalm xcii, where the context makes it plain that the word should have read 'palm-tree', another meaning of the original Hebrew word. Similarly, in the Authorized Version of the Book of Job, xxix. 18, the word 'sand' replaces 'phoenix' which appears in the Septuagint.

Stories of this bird go back as far as the eighth century B.C., and achieved widespread popularity. The phoenix was recognized as a symbol of the sun, and it is likely that the legends originated in Egypt, being connected in some way with heathen religious rites.

The unfortunate phoenix was condemned to a life of permanent celibacy, for there was never more than one at a

time. Shakespeare, perhaps pitying its solitary state, paired
it with a female dove, but most early authorities indicate that
it had no mate and did not couple with birds of other
species. Usually it is regarded as male, but one version of the
story asserts that each phoenix was of the opposite sex to its
predecessor, the male bird killing its female parent and
vice versa.

Perhaps its celibate state accounted for its longevity, for
although sexual arousal was said to prove beneficial by
stimulating the brain, the ejaculation of sperms was considered to have an adverse effect because it shortened the
life. Be that as it may, the phoenix lived for a very long
time, more than twelve thousand years in some versions of
the legend, though only for five hundred years in the
opinion of most authorities.

There was nothing new in the convenient idea of par-
thenogenesis, or the female virgin birth. After all, maidens
had been attesting the truth of that phenomenon ever since
the human race began. Yet the phoenix demonstrated a
much rarer phenomenon, namely that of the male which,
without any assistance from the female, managed not only
to beget but also to conceive its own offspring. The precise
manner in which it performed this remarkable feat is left to
our imagination.

Herodotus' account of the way in which the dead phoenix
was wrapped in myrrh and conveyed by its offspring to the
Temple of the Sun at Heliopolis is quoted in chapter one
of this book. Pliny offers a rather different version of the
story, for he asserted that the phoenix had a premonition of
its own approaching death and would build for itself a nest
of spices in which it died. The young phoenix sprang to life
from the corpse of the parent bird in the form of a tiny worm
which within three days became a fully fledged phoenix and
carried the remains of the parent-bird, still enclosed in its
coffin of spices, to the Temple of the Sun for cremation.

The version of the death of the phoenix as it appears in
the *Physiologus* represents a further variation. Here the bird
flies to Heliopolis and burns itself to death on the altar.
From among the ashes a tiny worm emerges, developing

into a phoenix which flies away on the third day. Alternatively it was believed that the bird built itself a nest of spices which was ignited by the hot rays of the sun, whereupon the phoenix would commit suicide by fanning the flames with its own wings until it was burnt to death. There were obvious parallels in these stories with the Resurrection, and the bestiary writers exploited these to the full.

By the sixteenth century the legend had been expanded, and men now believed that there was only one tree, located in Arabia, where the phoenix could build its nest.

Sir Thomas Browne was frankly sceptical about the whole business. He pointed out that few of the ancient writers claimed actually to have seen the phoenix with their own eyes, and that in any event other birds were often mistaken for it. The bird of paradise was a typical subject of this sort of error, and its feathers often found their way into museums or other collections in mistake for those of the phoenix. Though a great rarity to the European, the bird of paradise was common in its native habitat, and ought not to have been confused with the phoenix, the sole representative of its species. As to the longevity of the phoenix, the authorities were in open disagreement, and it was difficult to see how any sort of conclusion could possibly be reached in respect of a bird which hardly anyone had ever seen.

Another formidable objection raised by Browne was a religious one, for he saw in the concept of one bird as the sole living representative of its species a deliberate contravention of God's command to all living things to 'be fruitful and multiply'. Its alleged reproduction without intercourse with a female of the species violated the laws of nature and usurped the prerogative given only to plants of genesis without sexual commerce.

Even Adam, regarded by some people as a hermaphrodite, could not propagate himself, and had to depend on a miracle to supply him with a companion. The fact that the helpmeet provided for him by God was female seemed to Browne highly significant, and conclusive proof that her function was a sexual one, for surely another man would have been much more valuable as a companion in any other context:

... and therefore God said, 'It is not good that man should be alone, let us make an helpmeet for him;' that is, an help unto generation; for as for any other help, it had been fitter to have made another man.

As to the idea that the phoenix emerged from a worm which was a kind of corruption of the parent-bird, this seemed to Browne an anomaly which was highly unnatural. For though, along with most of his contemporaries, he held the belief that some creatures were capable of 'begetting themselves at a distance, and as it were at second hand', as in the case of butterflies, silkworms, etc., he considered that generation of these species proceeded from what he called a 'specifical and seminal diffusion, retaining still an Idea of themselves, though it act that part a while in other shapes'. What is more, he contended that if God had intended men to reproduce in this fashion they would have felt as strong an attachment to the lice which bred on them as to their own children; while the rotting carcasses of the dead would have been capable of repopulating the entire world.

A great mystery surrounded the birth of another fabulous creature, the basilisk. In Pliny's day this reptile was regarded as a particularly terrifying snake, so venomous that it was capable of putting all other serpents to rout. Its name meant 'king of serpents' both in Greek and in Latin, and it was instantly recognizable by its mode of advancing with the front part of its body erect, instead of wriggling along the ground like other snakes.

So powerful was the venom of the basilisk that, according to Pliny, a mounted man who killed a basilisk by running his spear through it was himself killed instantly and his horse with him by the power of the venom rising up through the weapon.

Setting fire to bushes or breaking up rocks and stones by simply breathing on them, and killing people by giving off a foul stench were among the other less attractive social habits of this beast. In addition it could kill a man just by fixing its eye upon him. Some authorities claimed for it the power of death by priority of vision. This means that if the basilisk saw a man before he perceived it, the man would die, whereas if the man saw the basilisk first, it was the basilisk that would die.

Nevertheless, the human race was not entirely without protection against the basilisk, for it had one deadly enemy—the cockerel. Hearing its crow was enough to send the basilisk into a fit of convulsions from which it never recovered. According to Aelian, the gossipy Roman writer, travellers across the deserts of North Africa would take a cockerel along with them as a protection against the basilisk. Another effective safeguard was to hold up in front of it a transparent crystal vase, in order to mesmerize the animal as it raised its head, for the venom being thrown back in its throat would cause its instant death.

Gradually over the centuries the legend of the basilisk began to change and expand, so that by the Middle Ages men's idea of it had undergone a complete revolution. Under the influence of the powerful medieval imagination, miraculous tales began to circulate about the conception and birth of this strange creature.

It was thought that when cockerels were about seven years old they became impotent. Being now incapable of seminal ejaculation, they amassed sperms under the midriff. Gradually these deposits formed into a yellow egg which had no shell, but which was covered instead with a tough membrane to protect it against the roughest blows. Not surprisingly this egg caused acute pain to the cock, which nevertheless eventually managed to scratch a hole in the ground and lay it.

Some authorities asserted that the warmth of the mud in which the cock had laid its was sufficient to incubate it, but others claimed that this egg was 'adopted' by a most extraordinary foster parent—the toad. For apparently the toad by some special instinct was able to sniff out the seminal disorders of the aging cock, and would keep a close watch on it from a nearby hiding place. Having observed the cock scratching a hole in a dunghill, and laying its egg there, the toad would immediately take over the task of sitting on the egg until it was hatched.

Whether the offspring of this extraordinary male virgin

birth was incubated by the warmth of the mud or dung, or hatched by a toad, most people were agreed that what eventually emerged from the cock's egg looked like a cockerel in front and a serpent behind (Plate 10). Some bestiary accounts state that as soon as it is hatched the basilisk scuttles away to some old cistern or similar hiding place for fear of meeting its death by priority of vision. Meanwhile any tree which it happened to touch would lose its capacity for bearing fruit, while birds which flew into its range of vision would be killed instantly by the venom of its glance.

It has been suggested * that the idea of the basilisk being hatched from the egg of a cock may have arisen from the Septuagint rendering of Isaiah, which may be literally translated: 'They break the eggs of adders and weave the spider's web: he who would eat of their eggs, having crushed the wind-egg, finds in it a basilisk.'

During the early part of the fourteenth century the term *basilicoc* came into use. This was a borrowing from the French, and it can be seen that this French word accorded well with the notion of the basilisk's connection with the cock. Later, as a further development, the word cockatrice was identified with the word basilisk, or basilicoc, and by the sixteenth century these words had come to be regarded as interchangeable. All the characteristics of these two beasts were now fully shared. Thus Trevisa, in his translation of Bartholomew Anglicus, gives an account of the engendering of the cockatrice: 'A for-lyued cok leyeth egges in his last elde . . . and yf any venimous worme sitteth on brood thereupon in the canicular days, thereof is gendrid . . . a cockatrice.'

The unicorn, like the basilisk, features in the Septuagint, and its appearance there has given rise to a great deal of speculation, which goes on even today, as to whether or not a real animal or an imaginary one was intended.

One of the most popular theories is that the reference in question was really to the rhinoceros. So far as the Bible is concerned, however, the unicorn is noted as a sacrificial animal in one chapter (Isaiah, xxxiv. 7), whereas in Jewish ceremonial ritual the unicorn would have been considered

* Robin, p. 87.

ineligible, because it did not fulfil the essential qualification
of being a cloven-footed ruminant.

Though Herodotus mentions the unicorn, it is Ctesias the
Greek who gives us the first full account of this animal. In
his *Indica* he describes it as approximately similar in build to
the horse, with a white body, purple head and dark blue
eyes. The long horn affixed to the centre of its brow was
white at the base, black in the centre and dark red at the tip.
Though it ran slowly at first, it rapidly increased its speed,
and as it gathered momentum could gallop like the wind,
rapidly outstripping the fastest horses. As a consequence
of its superior swiftness it could be captured only when
grazing in the meadow with its young.

Lewes Vertomannus, an Italian who journeyed to Arabia
and Egypt in 1503, disagrees with this account of the
dramatic colouring of the unicorn, and gives a very different
description:

This beast is of the colour of a horse of weesell colour,
and hath the head like a hart, but no long neck, a thynne
mane hanging only on the one side. Their leggs are thin and
slender like a fawn or hind. The hoofs of the fore-feet are
divided in two, much like the feet of a goat. The outer part
of the hinder feet is very full of hair. This beast doubtless
seemeth wild and fierce, yet tempereth that fierceness with
a certain comeliness.

Father Jerome Lobo, a seventeenth-century Portuguese
Jesuit, disagreed with Vertomannus in regard to both the
unicorn's mane and its temper. He writes: 'Some have long
manes hanging to the ground. They are so timorous that
they never feed but surrounded with other beasts that
defend them.'

Aelian gives yet another version of their disposition:

It has, of all animals, the harshest and most contentious
voice. It is said to be gentle to other beasts approaching it,
but to fight with its fellows. Not only are the males at
variance in natural contention amongst themselves, but they
also fight with the females, and carry their combats to the
length of killing the conquered; for not only are their bodies
generally indued with great strength, but also they are armed
with an invincible horn. It frequents desert regions and

wanders alone and solitary. In the breeding season it is of gentle demeanor to the female, and they feed together; when this has passed and the female has become gravid, it again becomes fierce and wanders alone.

Most writers were agreed that the unicorn was in fact a very fierce beast. According to Isidore of Seville it was 'mortall enimy to the Olephant'. A sixth-century Alexandrian merchant called Cosmas states that the unicorn cannot be captured because of its great ferocity, and that its strength is in its horn, adding: 'When it finds itself pursued and in danger of capture, it throws itself from a precipice, and turns so aptly in falling, that it receives all the shock upon the horn and so escapes safe and sound.'

Though its fierce nature and powerful horn made the unicorn virtually unassailable, the hunter could overcome it by two strategies.

The first of these was to position himself in front of a large tree and goad the beast into a charge. Provided that the hunter sidestepped successfully at the crucial moment, the unicorn would find itself unable to check its impetus in time, and with head lowered would run headlong into the tree. The force of its own charge would embed the horn deeply in the trunk, and the animal would be unable to withdraw. At this juncture the huntsman could safely approach and cut off its head.

The other strategy seems to have developed in medieval times, and the first known reference to it is to be found in a four-volume treatise called *Physica* written in a Benedictine convent near Bingen between 1156 and 1160 by the Abbess Hildegard. In this book she explains that the unicorn could be captured only by beautiful young virgins who had led pure lives, and on whom the unicorn would gaze adoringly, oblivious of everything else. A century later a German canon called Konrad von Megenberg, in *Das Buch der Natur*, added that the unicorn would be so awed by the purity of the maiden that it would lay its head in her lap.

The unicorn therefore became a symbol of purity, and it was common for medieval painters to portray saints or even the Virgin Mary with unicorns.

Despite this reputation for purity, hints of the unicorn's sexuality began to creep in, and underlie many medieval accounts. In some pictures the virgin is actually nude, as in the bestiary illustration shown in Plate 15. Here the unicorn, lying with his eyes closed and his head in the lap of his naked maiden, certainly has a very strange, self-satisfied smirk. The account given in chapter five of this book, of a similar ruse employed to catch elephants in Ethiopia, notes how the elephant enjoys licking the teats of nude maidens. It is probable that the two stories spring from a common source. An account given in Gerard Legh's book, *The Accedens of Armorie*, sheds a further light on the nature of the unicorn's attachment to maidens and what actually passed between them:

> When he [the unicorn] is hunted he is not taken by strength, but onely by this policie. A maid is set where he haunteth, and shee openeth hir lap, to whome the Unicorne ... yeeldeth his head, and leaueth al his fiercenes, and resting himselfe vnder her protection, sleepeth vntill he is taken and slain. . . .

The expression 'to lie in the lap' used to be a euphemism for sexual intercourse, as the following piece of dialogue from the 'players' scene' in *Hamlet* illustrates:

HAMLET Ladye, shall I lie in your lap?
OPHELIA No, my lord.
HAMLET I mean, my head vpon your lap?
OPHELIA Ay, my lord.
HAMLET Do you think I meant country matters?
OPHELIA I think nothing, my lord.
HAMLET That's a fair thought to lie between maids' legs.*

Even in seventeenth-century England the horn of the unicorn was a great curiosity. John Tradescant senior, creator of the first English 'arch of novelties', was said to have exhibited a horn, believed to be that of a unicorn, in court circles during the year 1632. After much deliberation, however, it was pronounced merely 'the snout of a fish, yet very precious against poisons'. For besides being a great novelty, the unicorn horn was said to possess special

* Act III, Sc. 2.

medicinal and curative properties, acting as a powerful aphrodisiac and as an infallible antidote to poison.

According to John Leo,* the horn of the unicorn was about three feet long, and smooth and white like ivory. Other animals, knowing its efficacy against poison, would delay drinking from a stream or fountain until the unicorn had dipped its horn in the water. A famous tapestry, 'The Unicorn at the Fountain', one of a set of French or Flemish tapestries dating from about the end of the fifteenth century, shows this happening (Plate 13).

Aelian was the first writer to describe the spiral twist of the 'unicorn' horn, which was later adopted in heraldry. The narwhal, which is sometimes called the sea-unicorn, has a long tusk which is twisted in this way. These, and the horns of the rhinoceros or other animals, were often either genuinely mistaken for the horns of unicorns, or were fraudulently offered for sale under that name.

For there was scope for huge profit in the sale of these horns. Every self-respecting chemist or apothecary had his own supply, from which he could compound at will the various essential remedies, and during the sixteenth and seventeenth centuries the unicorn horn was frequently found on apothecaries' signboards, where it acted as a reassuring indication both of the skill of the proprietor and of the value of his stock.

When pounded down to a fine powder the horn could either be swallowed on its own or added to other minerals and simples, according to the patient's individual requirements. People usually preferred to take the powder with food or drink, for it stuck to the tongue and sometimes had an unpleasant, earthy taste, perhaps because it was often found buried in the soil with other animal bones. Though the unicorn horn was most famous as a remedy for poison and as an aphrodisiac, it had many other uses. Valentini, a German doctor of the early eighteenth century, who wrote a book called *Natur- und Materialienkammer*, said that pre-

---

* The works of this Arab scholar and traveller were translated into English under the titles *Navigazione e viaggi* (trans. G. B. Ramusio, London, 1550) and *Historie of Africa* (trans. J. Pory, London, 1600).

1. The opening page of *The Royal Bestiary*. It deals with the definition of the word 'beast', and then proceeds to the lion.

Incipit lib de naturis bestiaꝝ. ⁊ earum significa
eſtiarū uoca tionibꝫ.
bulum ꝓprie auenit
leonibꝫ pardiſ ⁊ tigbꝫ
lupiſ ⁊ uulpibꝫ. cam
bus ⁊ ſimiis. vrſibꝫ
⁊ cetis que uł ore uł
unguibꝫ ſeuiunt ex
ceptiſ ſerpentibꝫ. Beſ
tie aūtē dicte auꝫ q̄
ſeuiunt. fere appella
te eo q̄o naturali utuntū libertate. ⁊ deſiderio
ſuo feruntū Sunt eñi libere coꝝ uoluntates ⁊
huc atꝗ; illuc uagantū. Et quo animuſ dirre
rit: eo ferantur. De naturis Leonuꝙ.

2. Huntsmen who stole tiger cubs were relentlessly pursued by the tigress, who could be tricked by throwing down a glass ball: she would at first mistake her reflection for her cub, thus giving the huntsman time to escape. From *The Royal Bestiary*.

ꞁꞷꞇꞇꞙ ꞃꞷꞃꜻꞇꜻ ꞃꞃꞇꝺ ꞹꞷꞁꞷꜻꞇꞑ̃ ꞓꞷꞃꝼ̃. ꞇꞇꜻ ꝺꝺ . ꞃꞷ

3. The dragon was a fierce enemy of the elephant, and would ambush it, leap onto its back and fetter its feet with its coils. From *The Royal Bestiary*.

4. The whale was difficult to draw because its appearances were so rare.
From *The Royal Bestiary*.

5. The title page of *The Historie of Foure-footed Beastes.*

THE
HISTORIE
OF
FOVRE-FOOTED
BEASTES.

Defcribing the true and liuely figure of euery Beaft, with a difcourfe
of their fuerall Names, Conditions, Kindes, Vertues (both naturall and
medicinall) Countries of their breed, their loue and hate to Mankinde, and the
wonderfull worke of God in their Creation, Preferuation,
and Deftruction.

Neceffary for all Diuines and Students, becaufe the ftory of euery Beaft is amplified with Narrations out of Scrip-
tures, Fathers, Phylofophers, Phyfitians, and Poets : wherein are declared diuers Hyeroglyphicks, Emblems,
Epigrams, and other good Hiftories, Collected out of all the Volumes of CONRADVS GESNER, and all
other Writers to this prefent day.   By EDWARD TOPSELL.

The   Gorgon

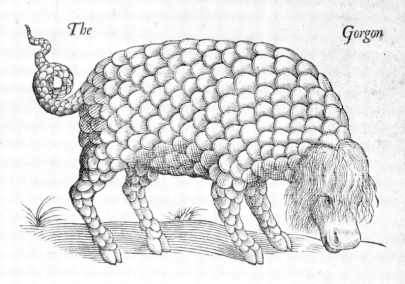

LONDON,
Printed by William Iaggard.
1 6 0 7.

6. The manticore. From *The Royal Bestiary*.

7. The manticore. From *The Historie of Foure-footed Beastes*.

8. The 'true picture of the Lamia'. From *The Historie of Foure-footed Beastes*.

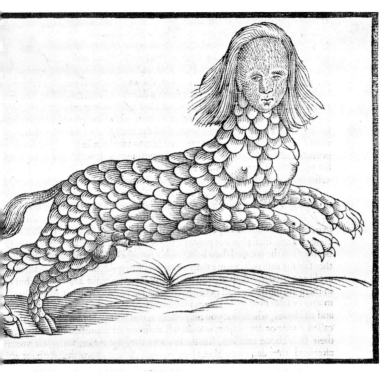

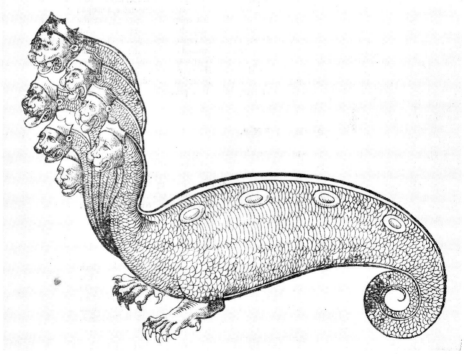

9. The hydrus. From *The Historie of Foure-footed Beastes*.

11. Centaur; detail of a French twelfth-century carving.

parations made from these horns acted as a neutralizing agent for excess acid in the blood and were very efficacious against diarrhoea.

Nevertheless Valentini was one of the growing number of sceptics of his era who did not believe in the existence of unicorns. The widespread use of the horns in apothecaries' shops was in his view a convincing argument against the existence of this so-called rare animal. Yet many people continued not only to believe in them but also to swallow these strange concoctions, and line the pockets of the apothecaries.

Often people tried to carry out crude experiments to find out whether horns which they found belonged to the unicorn. The explorer Frobisher, for instance, reports how a group of sailors discovered a large hollow horn on the beach. This horn had a spiral twist, and there is little doubt that what they had really stumbled upon was a tusk of the narwhal. Yet to find out whether it was a genuine unicorn horn, they placed several spiders inside it, the latter being regarded as extremely poisonous. When these died, it seemed to the sailors positive proof that what they had found was a unicorn horn.

Sometimes unicorn horns were used as drinking vessels, particularly by royalty, who were all too often haunted by the fear of being poisoned by a jealous rival. The price that could be fetched by a good specimen could therefore be almost astronomical. Venice tried to buy one in the year 1559 for 30,000 ducats, a king's ransom in those days. The offer was rejected. Six years later King Frederick II of Denmark used one as a security against a huge loan with which he purchased the military supplies which were essential for his war against Sweden. As soon as the Treaty of Stettin was negotiated in 1570 he was careful to redeem it. A unicorn horn at Somerset House which was valued at £500 occurs in the inventory of King Charles I, while in Shakespeare's time there existed at Windsor Castle one which was 'above eight spans and a half in length, valued at more than £10,000'.

Tales of the unicorn flourished, therefore, in spite of the

scorn of the sceptics. At Swedenburg in Germany during the year 1663 a heap of bones together with a large horn believed to belong to a unicorn was unearthed. Among those present when the horn was dug up was the mayor of the nearby town of Magdeburg, and his imagination was so captured by the discovery that he tried to reconstruct the skeleton. Partly because it was put together on the false assumption that it must resemble known descriptions of the unicorn, the result was extraordinary, but as far as we know this was the oldest recorded attempt at a palaeontological reconstruction.

Another horned animal which, like the unicorn, was later to achieve considerable popularity as a heraldic device was the eale, or yale. In the bestiaries it is described as a black animal of about the same size as a horse, with a tail like an elephant's and the jowls of a boar. Its most remarkable characteristic is a pair of long horns which are not fixed but can swivel in any direction quite independently of each other. These are a great asset to the yale when it is fighting with other beasts, for it lays one horn along its back and points the other forward at its enemy, and if the front horn is blunted or deflected it brings the rear horn instantly into action (Plate 24).

The body of the yale varies in the bestiary illustrations, in some examples having the thickset form of the bull and in others the graceful outline of the antelope. Sometimes it has a pair of short tusks like a wild boar's, and often a goatish jaw and beard into the bargain. According to Pliny, the first known writer who described this beast, the yale is built on the same broad proportions as the hippopotamus or river horse, and it is said to have been equally at home either on land or in the water. Since it comes from Ethiopia, the usual home of monstrosities in early western literature, and is featured in a chapter dealing with strange composite animals, it is possible that Pliny actually regarded it as a cross between some sort of horned animal and the hippopotamus.

Closely related to the yale is the centichora, a native of India described by a French bestiarist as one of the cruellest of beasts, with horns more than four arms in length and sharper than spears. Like the yale, it places one horn lengthwise along its back when fighting, and uses the other, in the middle of its forehead, to kill its opponent.

The centichora has a barrel-shaped muzzle, thighs and breast like a lion's, the body and feet of a horse, an elephant's tail and the voice of a man. One writer claims that its eyes are very close together, and that it has huge ears which grow in place of teeth. Its deadliest enemy is the basilisk, which poisons it with a prick between the eyes when it is asleep, causing it to swell up in an alarming fashion until its eyes pop out of its head and the poor beast dies.

Sometimes the yale was confused with the catoblepas, an animal which many experts identify with the gnu, though it seems to possess some characteristics which accord with those of the hippopotamus. Aelian says that it is like a bull, yet crueller and more terrible, with thick black eyebrows and small bloodshot eyes which are almost always cast downwards. A thick mane of hair falls over its eyes, partly covering its face and rendering it all the more terrifying. Its habit of keeping its head lowered on account of its great weight was normally considered a good thing, for most authorities were agreed that the catoblepas could kill with a glance. Aelian elaborates this, claiming, however, that it kills not with its gaze but with its venomous breath.

It feeds on deadly herbs, and as soon as it has caught sight of anyone with its bull-like gaze, immediately it bristles up, and erects its mane, and with the mane raised aloft and with its mouth open, it ejects from its throat something of a most deadly and poisonous nature, so that the air above its head is clouded with it and infected; animals coming near, which breathe the air are seriously overcome, lose their voice, and fall down in fatal convulsions, which also, they say, happens to a man. This wild beast knows that it has this noxious power in itself, and other living creatures know it too, and keep away from it as far as possible.

The history of dragons in western literature is not easy to establish, because the word 'dragon' was often used by classical writers to describe ordinary snakes. When, for instance, Pliny names dragons as the traditional enemy of the elephant and tells how they lurk in the branches of high trees waiting to pounce on passing elephants, hoping to crush them to death in their coils, he is probably referring to pythons (Plate 3). The crested forehead and sharp teeth noted by Bartholomew Anglicus, however, would seem to indicate that he had real dragons in mind:

The dragon is most greatest of all serpents, and oft he is drawn out of his den, and riseth up into the air, and the air is moved by him, and also the sea swelleth against his venom, and he hath a crest with a little mouth, and draweth breath at small pipes and straight, and reareth his tongue, and hath teeth like a saw, and hath strength, and not only in his teeth, but also in his tail, and grieveth both with biting and with stinging, and hath not so much venom as other serpents: for to the end to slay anything, to him venom is not needful, for whom he findeth he slayeth, and the elephant is not secure of him, for all his greatness of body.

The idea of the winged, scaly dragon with its cruel mouth and sharp teeth, breathing fire and puffing smoke through its nostrils, is largely a medieval conception. In Herodotus' day dragons were shaped like serpents with wings, and sometimes had a crested brow. Heredotus himself claimed to have seen the remains of these flying serpents in Arabia:

I went once to a certain place in Arabia, almost exactly opposite the city of Buto, to make enquiries concerning the winged serpents. On arrival I saw the black bones and ribs of serpents in such numbers as it is impossible to describe: of the ribs there were a multitude of heaps, some great, some small, some middle sized. The place where the bones lie is at the entrance of a narrow gorge between steep mountains, which there open upon a spacious plan communicating with the great plain of Egypt. The story goes, that with the spring the winged snakes come flying from Arabia towards Egypt, but are met in this gorge by birds called ibises, who forbid their entrance and destroy them all. The Arabians assert, and the Egyptians also admit, that it is on account of this service thus rendered that the Egyptians hold the ibis in so much reverence.

Present-day tourists to Egypt may see abundant evidence

of the reverence in which the ibis was once held. In ancient Egyptian burial grounds not far from Cairo, rows upon rows of sacrificed ibis birds may be seen. Each one is carefully wrapped in a linen shroud and placed in an individual clay pot, filed, as it were, for eternity. Pilgrims from far and near used to offer these birds just as today in another religion they might light a candle.

Besides being kept down by the fierce attacks of the ibis, the dragon population was severely limited by its own strange sexual habits, for in the middle of copulation the female would suddenly kill her mate by biting off his head. In due course the process of procreation would bring about the death of the mother also, for the offspring, instead of waiting to be ejected from the womb by natural labour, would bite their way out through the belly of their dam.

Unlike most other animals mentioned in the bestiaries, the dragon is not featured separately, but instead is noted only in relation to other animals. It is therefore only described as attacking its mortal enemy, the elephant, or flying from the sweet but deadly breath of the panther, or lying in wait for doves under the peridexion tree.

By the Middle Ages the dragon had come to be regarded as the embodiment of all that was evil, and attracted a series of famous legendary heroes who overcame it in single combat. The dragon in *Beowulf* is the oldest example in English literature, and this account, written in the last quarter of the eighth century, details a dragon which was serpentine in appearance. A similar snake-like shape is given in some of the earlier illustrations to the legend of St George and the Dragon, though by the later Middle Ages the beast had attained the shape familiar to modern readers. Probably heraldry, with its fixed rules, tended to assist in the process of regularizing the outline, in the form now generally accepted.

Most people will be familiar with the legendary characteristics of the dragon, which were, of course, taken very seriously in the Middle Ages. One of its less well advertised but nevertheless highly disconcerting habits was that of flying by night and urinating on the populace below. Men thought that if dragon's water fell upon them, their skin would immediately putrefy. Some people even maintained that the affected parts would actually drop off.

Perhaps it is hardly surprising that stories of this kind were invented. For mankind was afflicted by a series of terrible epidemics, which reached a climax in the Middle Ages. Leprosy, still a scourge in some parts of the world, with its disastrous wasting effect on all parts of the body, must have seemed a mysterious and terrifying disease which somehow had to be explained. Another dreaded disease whose symptoms would have corresponded even more closely with the alleged effects of dragon's water was St Anthony's fire, a type of erysipelas caused by a growth of fungus on rye, which was the staple bread of the poor in medieval Europe.

The disease began with sensations of extreme cold in the affected parts, followed by burning. Just as in the stories about the dragon's urine, the flesh then putrefied and the diseased part dropped off. After the damaged limb had fallen from the body, the sufferer usually recovered, and it was not uncommon for people to survive the loss of all four limbs, though the kind of existence which would have been possible under such circumstances in an age of poverty and ignorance must have been almost unbearable.

During the course of a major epidemic of St Anthony's fire, a hospital with a church attached was set up at Vienne in the eleventh century. Serious attempts were made to cure the sufferers, and those people whose affected parts did not drop off of their own accord had them amputated. These putrid, blackened, severed limbs were then hung in the church without any kind of embalming or other preservative treatment.

Overcrowding, poor sanitation, rotten food and inadequate standards of hygiene were often the causes of the various epidemics of the Middle Ages. Divine punishment, movement of the stars, and even the poisoning of wells by the Jews were commonly blamed for these outbreaks. It is perhaps hardly surprising that the urine of the dragons, symbolic of the devil in the Middle Ages, was also considered to be the cause.

According to Bartholomew Anglicus, dragons often band together in packs of four or five. Fastening their tails together and rearing up their heads they sail over rivers and oceans in search of good meat. Because dragons are permanently afflicted with a burning thirst, they have an overwhelming desire for the elephant's blood on account of its coldness:

> Jerome saith, that the dragon is a full thirsty beast, insomuch that unneth he may have water enough to quench his great thirst; and openeth his mouth therefore against the wind, to quench the burning of his thirst in that wise. Therefore when he seeth ships sail in the sea against the wind, he flieth against the sail to take their cold wind, and overthroweth the ship sometimes for greatness of body, and strong rese against the sail. And when the shipmen see the dragon come nigh, and know his coming by the water that swelleth ayenge him, they strike the sail anon, and scape in that wise.

The griffin, or gryphon, is chiefly known to the modern reader as a heraldic beast featured in many coats of arms, and also because Lewis Carroll wrote about it in *Alice's Adventures in Wonderland*, where it is depicted in Sir John Tenniel's illustrations. Its popularity in medieval times stems very largely from the fact that it played an important role in the legend of Sinbad the sailor, which then had an amazing vogue.

Bartholomew Anglicus describes the griffin as a four-footed beast with wings, 'like to the lion in all parts of the body, and to the eagle only in the head and wings'. In some descriptions the forelegs also resembled those of the eagle.

The griffin was very partial to human flesh, and it could easily tear a man to pieces with its cruel talons. Nevertheless its own flesh was unpalatable and men could not eat it. So large were its claws that if you were lucky enough to come by one you could use it as a drinking horn. Yet the griffin had one powerful enemy, the lion, against whom it waged continual war, and it was on account of the lion's hostility that the griffin selected for its lair a cave with a very narrow entrance. The lion had a special capacity for smelling out the eggs of the griffin, yet it could not penetrate the narrow entrance to the lair, and eggs could therefore safely be laid there. The mountains where it had its nests were reputed to contain vast hoards of precious stones, which the griffin guarded so fiercely that nobody could carry them away.

The strength of the griffin was phenomenal. It was said to be fully capable of carrying off a horse or even an elephant in its talons. An account of the beast is given in *Mandeville's Travels*:

In that contre aryn grefonys manye, that han the forme of the egele byfore and the forme of the lyoun byhynde. But a greffoun there is more and strengere than viii. lyonys of this contre and strengere than an hondered egellys here, for a grefoun hymself alone wele bere to his nest an hors with a man armyd on his bak, or too oxen yokede togedere to his nest. The naylis of hese feet aryn as meche as oxis hornys, and they make of hem coppys for to drynkyn of, as men don here of bugele hornys, and of the bakkis of here federes they make stronge bowis to shetyn therwith.

A curious marine creature which terrified mariners and hampered their passage across the oceans of the world was the serra, or saw-fish. In *The Bestiary of Philip de Thaun* it is described as a winged beast of the sea which has the head of a lion and the tail of a fish. When it perceives a ship it flies above it and attacks the vessel, meanwhile holding off the wind from the sail by placing itself strategically in such a position that the wind is diverted and the ship becalmed. To the bestiarist the serra signifies the devil, who withdraws from mankind the beneficial breeze of holy inspiration.

Even in the seventeenth century a school of thought still existed which maintained that every creature which lived and breathed on land had its counterpart in the depths of the ocean. The sea-unicorn, sea-horse, sea-satyr and sea-amphisbaena are just some of the real or imaginary counterparts of real or imaginary land animals.

Perhaps the most extraordinary of these fabulous marine

creatures is the bishop-fish, noted by Vincent de Beauvais. The bishop-fish was thought to resemble a bishop in almost every particular. In a book entitled *On Marine Fishes* written by the naturalist Rondeletius in the middle of the sixteenth century, there is a description of this strange creature accompanied by the author's own drawing. It stands erect on two legs, and is mitred and robed like a human bishop. Naturally, since there was a bishop-fish, there had to be a monk-fish also. The grave features and tonsured head are of this fish the most outstanding characteristics, but almost equally noteworthy are the wide tail which trails behind like a cassock, the arms with fins at the end, and the total absence of feet. The entire body except for the face and forehead is covered with scales.

These are some of the strange fabulous beasts that flourished in the imaginations of our ancestors. Yet if we are tempted to laugh at some of these mistaken notions, we should first consider the difficulties of observation and lack of scientific aids which handicapped mankind only a few centuries ago. If we consider the kind of information which we ourselves have gathered together within our own life-span, we will find that it is in fact a mixture of direct human experience and the reported findings of other people. Whether or not we decide to accept second-hand data depends to a large extent on the authority of the person from whom we receive them. Many people are still inclined to accept the view that anything which has appeared in print must be true, and this outlook is as dangerous now as it was in the days of our forefathers, who tended to believe that what was written down in manuscript books or what was explained by the fathers of the Church or the ancient classical writers was gospel truth.

And without reliable first-hand knowledge it must be admitted that many real beasts are as extraordinary as the imaginary ones, and in some cases even more so. Who, for instance, without other supporting data would accept the elephant, with its huge, clumsy body and long trunk and tusks in preference to the unicorn, which after all looked very much like an ordinary horse with a horn on its head?

As to the dragon or flying serpent, this was surely no more strange than the *Tyrannosaurus rex*, which scientists tell us was more than forty feet long, yet despite its great strength died from the face of our earth more than a hundred million years ago.

Today there are still stories in circulation concerning beasts which could be real or fabulous. Few people would, for example, care to deny positively the existence of the abominable snowman, that huge, shaggy, manlike creature said to terrify mountaineers in the region of the Himalayas. And despite all our modern amenities in terms of scientific instruments and versatile equipment for the recovery of large objects, added to the wealth of information at the disposal of our experts, we are still unable to establish whether or not there really is a monster living in the depths of Loch Ness. There are, of course, various theories about the objects which have been sighted in the water over a large number of years by many people. Perhaps they are decaying clumps of vegetation giving off bubble-producing gases. Alternatively they could be over-size otters disporting themselves in the water, to the utter confusion of the casual passer-by. Nor is it beyond the realms of possibility that there may be some strange survivor from the days when the earth was populated by dinosaurs. The depth and coldness of this stretch of water could possibly have preserved such a monster in an era when climatic changes and a variation in the vegetation of the earth deprived these monsters of their natural food. The plesiosaurus with its long thin neck and small head would certainly accord well with the outline of the object commonly seen in photographs.

Despite mankind's tremendous achievements in space, there are still areas of the earth which are largely unexplored and, curiously enough, we know more about large areas of the Moon's surface than we do about the North and South Poles. We cannot tell what strange beasts still remain to be discovered, and if we would dismiss the beliefs of mankind up to the middle of the seventeenth century as childish and absurd, we would do well to bear in mind the gaps which still exist in our own knowledge.

CHAPTER FOUR

Men as Beasts and Beasts as Men

AMONG the most intriguing categories of imaginary beasts included in the bestiaries and other religious writings which passed into the main stream of animal lore were the strange composite beasts, part animal and part human, largely derived from the legends of Greece and Rome and other ancient civilizations, and fantastic subhuman creatures with weird abnormalities. Travelogues from the earliest times helped to encourage widespread belief in creatures of these kinds, for whenever men ventured into the unknown they brought back thrilling tales of mysterious beasts. Since real animals were often as extraordinary as the imaginary ones, our ancestors can be forgiven for being unable to distinguish fact from fiction.

It is impossible to over-emphasize the influence of classical mythology on the mind of man. Stories from these sources spread throughout the Greek and Roman spheres of influence, sometimes enchanting and sometimes terrifying their hearers, but always making an irresistible appeal to the imagination. This is hardly surprising, for some of the world's greatest story-tellers, including Homer and Virgil, handed them down for posterity, ensuring for them a popularity which is never likely to decline as long as men read books.

Many of the curious creatures described in these tales had a religious significance in the multitheistic classical religions from which they derived. They were therefore readily absorbed into other religions with a similar multiplicity of gods which, like those of Greece and Rome, exhibited such human characteristics as benevolence, malevolence and petulance, with the result that people often felt under an obligation to cajole them with sacrifices. They ought not to have fitted in so readily with the Christian religion, but we have already seen in chapters one and two of this book how mythological beasts sometimes managed to find their way quite by accident into the various translations of the Bible.

Their presence in both the Old and the New Testaments was seized on with some relief in the early days of Christianity. For men who turned eagerly to the Christian religion nevertheless found it difficult to shake off overnight the pagan beliefs which had gripped their minds for so many centuries. At first there were frequent defections to the old religions and religious practices, and the occasional inclusion in Christian belief of a creature from the mythology of the past would have acted as a comforting link with former religious notions. One instance was the frequent Godiva-like rides of nude women on white steeds, not as acts of charity but as part of ancient fertility ceremonials in which whole villages often took part, despite the efforts made by the Church to stamp them out or hush them up. The survival of pagan rites in Christianity may be likened to preservation of their remnants, including fertility rites, in countless ancient customs. The use of mistletoe at Christmas is an example of one such custom which has survived up to the present day.

One creature which still tends to be associated primarily with classical mythology is the satyr. In pictures and carvings dating back to the classical era it is usually portrayed as an elementary pastoral figure, often playing on a reed pipe. Although it possesses the calm, gentle features of a youth, it is nevertheless the horned forehead, goatlike hooves and tail which furnish the real clue to its character. For it derives its bestial nature from the lower half of its body, and is noted for its curious characteristic capers and lascivious behaviour. According to Pliny, its name is derived from the *membrum virile*, on account of its insatiable lecherous indulgences.

A special kind of Greek drama called the satyric derives

its name from this brute. The subject of the play was handled in a semi-comic fashion, and its special feature was a chorus made up entirely of satyrs. Unfortunately there are only two examples of this kind of play still in existence. One of these is by Euripides, and is entitled *Cyclops*, and the other, by Sophocles, is called *Ichneutae*.

The satyr is mentioned in the Authorized Version of Isaiah (xxxiv. 14) where it is used to render the Hebrew phrase '*s͢eʿīrīm*', which, strictly translated, means 'hairy ones': 'The wild beasts of the desert shall also meet with the wild beasts of the island, and the satyr shall cry to his fellow; and the screech owl also shall rest there, and find for herself a place of rest.'

Whether this allusion to the satyr is a mistranslation or faulty zoology is a matter for speculation. Alternatively, perhaps the writer of Isaiah was trying to emphasize the desolation of the scene by giving free rein to his own poetic fancy. Nevertheless because it was mentioned in the Bible the satyr was duly commented on by the early Christian fathers, and so eventually found its way into the bestiaries.

Evidence shows us that confusion used to arise between the mythological satyr and the great ape, known to Pliny as the satyrus, an animal of prodigious swiftness, which sometimes went on all fours and sometimes walked upright like a man. Topsell solemnly observed that satyrs 'had no human condition in them, nor other resemblance of man beside their shape; though Solinus speake of them like as of men. They carry their meat under their chin, as in a storehouse, and from thence being hungry they take it forth to eate, making it ordinary with them every day, which is but annuall in the Formicae lions.'

Lest the reader be misled into supposing that the Formicae lions were some sort of feline with a feast-day once a year, it should be added that they were actually tiny ants who annually laid by a store of grain to tide them over the winter.

As an example of the satyr's lustful disposition, Topsell, in *The Historie of Foure-footed Beastes*, relates an episode from the voyages of Ephemus Car, in which an account is given of an encounter with these beasts, described as red in colour and having a tail almost as large as that of the horse:

These being perceived by the Mariners to run to the Ships and lay hold on the women that were in them, the Ship-men for fear took one of the Barbarian women and set her on the land among them, whom in most odious and filthy manner they abused, not only in that part that nature hath ordained, but over the whole body most libidinously, whereby they found them to be very brute beasts. (Plate 19.)

When the satyr passed into the bestiaries it was often depicted in a lively illustration as a nude man with a beard, horned brow and long tail. Sometimes the legs and feet are human, sometimes goat-like. Usually it grasps in its hand some sort of phallic symbol, such as a writhing serpent or a knobbed staff (Plate 20). Occasionally it is also to be seen drinking from a wine cup.

If it seems strange to us now that men could seriously believe in beasts of this kind, we must remember how closely the satyr resembled another powerful claimant to the medieval imagination, the devil himself.

In the Authorized Version we find the same expression *sĕ'îrîm*, or 'hairy ones', which had been translated as 'satyr' in Isaiah rendered 'Devil' in Revelations: '. . . and the great dragon was thrown down, that ancient serpent who is called the Devil and Satan, the deceiver of the whole world.'

The devil, symbolically yet terrifyingly depicted as the dragon or serpent, has already been discussed in chapter two. But as well as being given this symbolic interpretation, he has also been conceived as a real person, usually possessing some or all of the characteristics of the satyr. Topsell points to this similarity in his *Historie of Foure-footed Beastes*: 'The satyr, a most rare and seldome seene Beast, hath occasioned others to thinke it was a Deuill'.

This conception of the devil as a real person who might appear at any moment is well described in a book called *Wonders of the Invisible World*, written by Cotton Mather in 1693:

Alas, the Devils, they swarm about us, like the Frogs of Egypt in the most Retired of our Chambers. Are we at our Boards? There will be Devils to tempt us to Sensuality. Are we in our Beds? There will be Devils to tempt us to Carnality. Are we in our Shops? There will be Devils to tempt us into dishonesty. Yea, though we get into the Church of God, there will be Devils to Haunt us in the very Temple itself, and there Tempt us to manifold Misbehaviours.

Although the devil often had a satyr-like appearance, he could also take on the form of an ordinary human being, perhaps by taking over a corpse, and changing at will from one body to another. This kind of activity is noted by dramatist Thomas Dekker, in *The Witch of Edmonton*, first printed in 1621:

> The Old Cadaver of some selfe-strangled wretch
> We sometimes borrow, and appear humane.
> The Carcase of some disease-slain strumpet,
> We varnish fresh, and wear as her first Beauty.
> Didst never hear? if not, it has been done.
> An hot luxurious Leacher in his Twines,
> When he has thought to clip his Dalliance,
> There has provided been for his embrace
> A fine hot flaming Devil in her place.

According to Topsell (1658), the devil sometimes appeared disguised as a fairy: 'These and such like stories and opinions there are of Phairies, which in my judgment arise from the praestigious apparitions of Devils, whose delight is to deceive and beguile the minds of men with errour . . .'

A favourite story was once in common circulation about a satyr-like creature that appeared to a holy hermit living in the desert. Most authorities accept that the holy man was St Paul the Hermit, who lived in a cave in the desert for 113 years, and wore nothing but palm leaves. Fortunately the climate was warm. For sixty years he was fed by an obliging crow, who brought him half a loaf every day.

The story of St Paul the Hermit was written by Jerome, a scholarly monk who produced the Vulgate version of the Bible. In old age Jerome attracted the attention of various high-born society ladies, who devoted themselves to him, and his relationships with them, although no doubt perfectly proper, caused something of a scandal in his own day.

Some people claim, however, that the man to whom the strange beasts appeared was St Anthony, an illiterate man who lived to the age of 105 years without ever washing his feet and, perhaps luckily for his fellow men, lived the life of a hermit. Though a holy and pious man, his life was one long struggle against the devil, who constantly tormented him with obscene visions.

Here is Sir John Mandeville's account of the strange brute and the hermit:

In the desert of that lond of Egip an holy ermyte mette onys with a beste forshapyn, for it had the shap of a man from the nouyl dou(n)ward and from thene vpward the shap of a got with sharpe hornys stondynge in the hed. The ermyte askyd hym in Godis name what he was, and the beste answerede and seyde, 'I am a creature that Crist made dedliche, and in this desert I dwelle and go for to gete myn sustenance.' The beste preiede hym that he wolde preye for hym to God, that for saluacion cam from heuene to erthe and was born of a virgine and suffered pascioun, thour whom we alle beleuyn and arn alle at his ordenaunce. And yit is that hed of that eche beste with the hornis holdyn and kept of Alysander for a mervayle.*†

It will be noted that the usual order of man above the navel and goat below is reversed in this instance.

Equalling the satyrs in lust and also figuring in classical mythology are the centaurs, notorious for lechery and rape. According to Chester, an English writer of the seventeenth century, they were man-eaters who 'Liv'd by human flesh

---

* Bodley version.

† In the desert of that country of Egypt a holy hermit once encountered a deformed beast having the form of a man from the navel down and from that point upwards the form of a goat with sharp horns rising from his head. The hermit asked him in the name of God what manner of beast he was, and the beast replied, 'I am a beast which Christ made deadly, and I live in this desert, roaming about in search of food.' The beast begged him to pray for him to God who came to earth from heaven bringing salvation, being born of a virgin and suffering Passion, through whom we all believe and live according to his ordinance. And the head of that same beast with the horns still exists and is kept as an object of curiosity at Alexandria.

and villanie'. Centaurs are divided into two types, the hippocentaur and the onocentaur. Sir John Mandeville rather quaintly adds a third, the hippopotamus. He had arrived at this conclusion by faulty etymology, for the prefix *hippo* is actually derived from the Greek word for 'horse', the word 'hippopotamus' simply meaning 'river-horse'.

The hippocentaur resembles a man above the navel and, as the name suggests, a horse from the navel down. It is often depicted on four legs, having an additional pair in which are held a bow and arrow, as in Plate 11. Isidore gives an account of the hippocentaur without the usual accompanying symbolism, and reports that when the horsemen of the Thessalonians rode into battle they so merged with their horses' bodies that they appeared to have a composite form, part man, part horse.

As Sagittarius in ecclesiastical art the hippocentaur probably originates from the sign of the zodiac which is often illustrated in calendars. In the bestiary of Philip de Thaun, a symbolic interpretation is found. Christ on earth is said to be typified by the human part of the hippocentaur, while the horse-like hindquarters are said (by some elusive process of logic which defies comprehension) to symbolize Christ's revenge on his Jewish betrayers. The bow signifies that when his body was struck upon the cross, his spirit departed to those he loved and who were waiting for him.

Like the hippocentaur, the onocentaur resembles a man above the navel, but below the navel it has the body of a wild ass, or onager. It makes its appearance in the Hebrew Bible, and the word 'onocentauri' is retained in the Vulgate version of Isaiah (XIII. 21). Aelian writes of it that 'it has a man's face surrounded by long hair; that its breasts project in front; that its shoulders, arms, elbows and hands, and its chest down to the loins are of human form; its back, flanks, belly and hind feet resemble an ass, but under the belly (at the flanks) it approaches to white'.

The onocentaur is not only likened in the moralizing of the bestiaries to men who 'speak well in front and ill behind', but is also condemned by St Jerome for being

seduced by illicit pleasures and base debauchery. This reputation for filthy lechery may derive from the writings of
Pliny, who describes the male onager as being so jealous
that it is unable to countenance the competition and
potential rivalry of its own male young, and consequently
mutilates the genital organs of its male offspring at birth.

The Greek physician Ctesias is believed to be the first
writer to describe the martichoras, or manticore, as Pliny
and many others called it. This beast, said to originate in
India, was believed to have a triple row of teeth meeting
like the teeth of a comb and reaching from ear to ear. Its
face and ears appeared human, its eyes were blue or grey
and its complexion was vermilion. The body was described
as hairy, and resembling that of a lion, both in size and in
appearance. With its scorpion-like tail it could loose the
stinging spines located there in much the same way that an
archer lets fly arrows from a bow. Its voice is reported by
Aristotle to be rather like a cross between a trumpet and a
reed pipe. Most ancient authorities attribute remarkable
swiftness to the martichoras, and note its insatiable appetite
for the flesh of human beings. According to Aelian, its name
derives from the Indian, and means 'man-eater'. Certain of
the characteristics of this extraordinary animal accord well
with those of the Bengal tiger.

Topsell, in his *Historie of Foure-footed Beastes*, has a most
remarkable illustration of the martichoras, or manticore, in
which he seems in some extraordinary way to anticipate the
typical Edwardian face (Plate 7).

Beasts such as the centaur and the martichoras overcame
men by their natural ferocity, brute force and fleetness of
foot. But there were other classes of fabulous creatures who
used sexual seductiveness to lure men to their doom.

One of the most interesting beasts in this category is the
lamia, which, like the centaurs, has its origins in Greek
mythology. Analogous with the vampire, the lamia was
connected with the lilith, described in some Jewish literature as Adam's first wife, and whose name derives from
Lilitu, the Assyrian goddess of the night.

The lilith and lamia were both particularly hostile to

children, and were alike in assuming the form of a beautiful woman in order to entice infants and men. The goddess Hera passionately hated Lamia because Hera's husband, Zeus, had fallen desperately in love with her. As an act of revenge Hera brought about the death of Lamia's children, and in so doing brought on the attacks of madness which led Lamia to snatch babies from their mothers' arms in order to kill and devour them.

Keats wrote a symbolic poem about an imaginary Lamia, described by him as a dazzling serpent:

> She was a gordian shape of dazzling hue,
> Vermilion-spotted, golden, green, and blue;
> Striped like a zebra, freckled like a pard,
> Eyed like a peacock, and all crimson barr'd;
> And full of silver moons, that as she breathed,
> Dissolv'd, or brighter shone, or interwreathed
> Their lustres with the gloomier tapestries—
> So rainbow-sided, touch'd with miseries,
> She seem'd at once, some penanced lady elf,
> Some demon's mistress, or the demon's self.

In order to beguile a mortal man with whom she had fallen in love, Keats's Lamia took on the shape of a beautiful woman. The story on which Keats based his poem is also recounted by Burton in his *Anatomy of Melancholy*. He describes how a young man met a fair gentlewoman who told him that 'if he tarry with her, he should hear her sing and play, and drink such wine as never any drank, and no man should molest him: but she, being fair and lovely, would live and die with him, that was fair and lovely to behold. The young man, a philosopher, otherwise staid and discreet, able to moderate his passions, though not this of love, tarried with her a while to his great content, and at last married her, to whose wedding, amongst other guests, came Appolonius; who, by some probable conjectures, found her out to be a serpent, a lamia; and that all her furniture was, like Tantalus' gold, described by Homer, no substance, but mere illusions. When she saw herself descried, she wept, and . . . vanished in an instant.'

Topsell, on the other hand, though he preceded Keats by

only two centuries, took the lamia very seriously, and included a picture of it in his *Historie of Foure-footed Beastes*. He described the lamia in the following terms: 'The hinde parts of this beast are like unto a goate, his fore legs like a beares, his upper parts like to a woman, the body scaled all over like a dragon . . . and by their fraud they overthrow men. For when as they see a man, they lay open their breastes, and by the beauty thereof entice them to come neare to conference, and so having them within their compasse, they devoure and kill them.' It is interesting that despite their apparent female seductiveness, Topsell regards them as distinctly male, and emphasizes this aspect, both in his description and also in his accompanying drawing (Plate 8).

So far the beasts described in this chapter have been exclusively male, but we now come to a creature which was definitely female, and beautiful, and used its beauty to ensnare men.

The *Physiologus* describes the gorgon as having lovely golden hair and a laughing, playful nature which sometimes gives place to episodes of furious raging among the mountains. 'And when the day of her longing comes she stands up and cries aloud, first like a lion and the other wild animals, then like a man, then like a herd of cattle, and then like a winged dragon, and she says, "Come to me and satisfy the desire of the flesh". And all who hear her come swiftly and look upon her. . . . But when they see her, then at once they die.'

According to the *Physiologus* there is, however, an enchanter who by a ruse is able to overcome the gorgon. For 'he can read in the stars the place of her abiding and wanders thither, enchanting her from afar'. Immediately the gorgon responds by crying in the language of all creatures, but when he approaches within earshot, the enchanter bids her to dig a hole and place her head inside it, so that he can come to her without risk of death. Then as she waits with her face hidden in the hole, he quickly approaches and cuts off her head. This he afterwards keeps in a special dish, finding it useful to ward off the attacks of his enemies, for by pulling it out and brandishing it in front of their eyes he is able to turn them instantly into stone.

This story has obvious connections with the ancient mythical tale of Perseus and the Gorgon's head. However, when we reach Jacobean times, we find Topsell (1607) using the word *Gorgon* as an alternative for the catoblepas, which he describes as 'a beast all set over with scales like a dragon, having no haire except on his head, great teeth like Swine, having wings to flie, and hands to handle, in stature betwixt a Bull and a Calfe'. Pliny uses the word *catoblepas* for the gnu, which he describes as having an extremely heavy head that usually hangs downwards. He adds that meeting the eyes of this beast is fatal to man.

There is some difference of opinion as to the nature of the sirens, which seem to have found their way into the bestiaries because they are mentioned in Isaiah: 'Sirens and demons shall dance in Babylon, and hedgehogs and onocentaurs shall dwell in their houses.'

Apparently regarded in the Middle Ages as synonymous with the sirens were harpies, which seem nevertheless to have had a somewhat different origin. The word 'harpy' derives from the Greek *harpyiai*, which means 'snatchers', for they were once regarded as ghosts which took the living to join the dead, hence their occasional appearance on the carvings of tombs. In Homer's *Odyssey* where they fulfilled this function they were simply winds. Homer relates that a harpy called Pordage, or Swiftfoot, was the dam of Achilles' horses, and that the west wind sired them. This may possibly mean that harpies were once regarded as part horse.

Jerome, commenting on the sirens in Isaiah, describes them as demons, or some sort of monster, or huge crested flying dragons. *Physiologus* accepts them, however, as the classical sirens, that is, woman above the waist and fowl below. Their technique is to enchant the ears of mariners, so that they are drawn irresistibly towards them from afar off, and ultimately lulled by the extraordinary sweetness of their song. When at length sleep has robbed the sailors of all power to defend themselves, the sirens descend upon them and tear them into pieces with their cruel talons. The bestiarists saw in this story a moral for those who allow themselves to be rendered insensible by the evils of worldly pleasures, theatricals, musical entertainments, etc.

The above description of the sirens' physical characteristics is roughly consistent with the description found in the *Metamorphoses* of Ovid * where they are noted as having the feathers and feet of birds and maidens' faces. By the twelfth century A.D., however, bestiary writers like Philip de Thaun were reporting different physical attributes. Though the siren still retains the form of a beautiful woman, she also possesses falcon's feet and the now more familiar tail of a fish. A thirteenth-century poem, *L'Image du Monde*, by Gautier de Metz, goes one stage further, and the siren now has the head and body of a maiden as far as the breasts, the lower parts of a fish and the wings of a bird. According to Isidore de Seville, the sirens have both wings and talons because love not only flies but also wounds.

The mermaid, or siren in fish form, is probably better known to the modern reader. It is based on the female figure of the classical triton, and it is usually illustrated as a woman above the navel and a fish with curved tail below. Often the mermaid is portrayed with a mirror in one hand, and this may possibly reflect the traditional pose of Venus rising from the sea, holding her long tresses in one hand and a glass in the other. There is a third-century mosaic pavement from a Roman villa at Halicarnassus which shows Venus in this way, rising from the water and supported by two mermaids. As with the harpy or bird siren, the technique of the mermaid is to render men insensible by the magnetic attractions of its song, and when they have been seduced in this way to attack and kill them without mercy.

Both mermaids and sirens customarily accompanied their singing with various musical instruments. Servius states of the three sirens in the *Aeneid* † that one sang, another played on the pipes, and a third on the lyre. Isidore de Seville endorses this, and his comment is repeated in many bestiaries, particularly the French. A thirteenth-century bestiary

* v. 552.
† v. 864.

of Picardy, for example, reports that the three kinds of sirens produce different sorts of music, one playing on the horn, another on the harp, whilst the other sings.

The mermaids and sirens have male counterparts in the mermen or tritons. Though not described in the bestiaries, they are sometimes to be found in church carvings. Pliny records an incident in which a triton was reported to have been seen playing on a shell. According to his description, nereids are covered all over with hair, even in those parts which closely resemble the human form. He also notes a strange creature, the man of the sea, which climbs aboard ships in the night and weighs them down so heavily that sometimes they even sink below the waves.

Not all these composite creatures were dangerous or hostile to man. The sphinx is a composite beast well known from ancient times. Perhaps it is most familiar because of the colossal recumbent statue of a sphinx at Giza, where it has the traditional form of a human being above the waist and a lion below. In this particular instance the features given to the beast are those of King Khaffre, of the fourth dynasty (*c.* 2550 B.C.), and in this the common custom of bestowing royal features on the face of the sphinx is followed. In Asia, where the popularity of the sphinx spread rapidly because of the Egyptian influence, the beast developed wings, and gradually over the course of the centuries underwent a change of sex, becoming female instead of male. It is the female form which predominates in Greek art, where the sphinx, often closely associated with the lion or griffin, achieved considerable popularity up to the end of the sixth century A.D. Usually it has a long wig dressed in layers, a much slimmer and more graceful shape than the Asiatic version, and beautiful wings with a curved form.

According to Greek mythology, the sphinx was a single female beast who gave men the option of answering her riddle or being devoured. Oedipus, who encountered her near her native Thebes, was the first man able to give her the correct answer, and as a result the sphinx committed suicide.

To Topsell (1607), however, the sphinx was no legend but a real beast with a rough brown hairy body resembling

an ape. According to him, 'the face is very round yet sharp
and piked, having the breasts of women, and their favour or
visage very much like them: In that part of their body which
is bare without hair, there is a certain red thing rising in a
round circle like a Millet seed, which giveth great grace and
comeliness to their colour, which in the middle part is
human. Their voice is like a mans but not articulate, sound-
ing as if one did speak hastily with indignation or sorrow'.
As in the case of the Lamia, Topsell regards this as a male
animal, despite its female breasts and visage (Plate 21).

Of the various subhuman tribes with weird abnormalities
Pliny wrote: 'These and similar varieties of the human race
have been made by the ingenuity of nature as toys for herself and marvels for us.' The bestiary writers' outlook was
different. As far as they were concerned, these tribes were
created by God specifically to illustrate for mankind some
particular point of moral and Christian doctrine, and if
these were not immediately apparent it was their duty to
find them and point them out.

The wodewose, or savage man, is an instance of a strange
subhuman creature whose habits were thought to provide
a moral lesson. Believed to inhabit the deserts of India, it
usually went naked unless able by its hunting exploits to
secure for itself a lion skin. The chief physical characteristic
of the savage man is a single horn in the centre of the forehead, and it is forced to live in trees on account of the
serpents, griffins and dragons which proliferate in these
desert regions. By tradition it was the enemy of the centaurs,
with whom it continually waged war, and this is said by the
bestiarists to signify the eternal conflict between the soul
and the flesh. Living in trees in order to avoid conflict is said
to signify the soul, which is peaceable and dislikes fighting.

A particularly intriguing race of subhumans are the
Astomi, reported by Megasthenes, a third-century B.C.
Greek historian and geographer, to be nomads inhabiting a
region of India near the source of the River Ganges. These
creatures are covered all over with fur, but notwithstanding
this they clothe themselves in outfits manufactured entirely
from cotton wool. They have no mouths at all, and live

wholly on the air they breathe, supplemented by the sweet
odours of fruit and flowers, with which they always plentifully supply themselves before undertaking any long
journeys, for fear of lacking scent. So delicate is their sense
of smell that they can easily be killed by an obnoxious
odour.

Bartholomew Anglicus too reports a race which, though
possessing a mouth, cannot open it. These people are
accounted tongueless, and are able to communicate only by
using sign language. They breathe and suck through a
single hole located in the middle of their breasts. Another
race possesses a mouth in the normal place, but this is so
tiny that nourishment can be obtained only by sucking it
through a narrow straw. Pliny writes of a bandy-legged
race called the Sciritae who have only holes for noses, like
snakes.

A race of men who are 'dismembered in the part where
the head is' features in the writings of Solinus. These are the
Blemyae, who have no head at all, and instead have eyes and
mouths located in their breasts. In French versions of the
Romance of Alexander these Blemyae are included among the
people conquered by Alexander. Here they are described as
golden in colour, and with beards growing from their
waists to their knees. Unable to speak except in barks are the
Cynocephali, a tribe said to number over 120,000 subhumans, all of whom had dogs' heads. These people supported themselves by hunting and fowling, using their nails
as weapons.

Longevity is sometimes said to be a remarkable feature of
subhuman tribes. One Indian race, the Pandae, were said to
have white hair in youth which turned black in old age.
Their life-span was 200 years, while the inhabitants of
Mount Athos, who lived 140 years, attributed their longevity to their diet of snakes' flesh, which kept their head
and clothes free from harmful creatures. Snake-bite could
of course be a problem, but in Africa the Psylli tribe
encountered no such difficulty, for they engendered in their
bodies poison which was deadly to snakes. Their wives'
fidelity was commonly tested by exposing their newly born

offspring to poisonous snakes, for snakes were thought not to avoid persons with the blood of adultery in them.

According to Eudoxus, an atronomer and physicist who was a pupil of Plato, the men of one tribe in the southern part of India have enormous feet, eighteen inches in length. By complete contrast the women of the same tribe have feet so tiny that they are known as Struthopodes, or Sparrow-feet. Yet abnormalities were sometimes thought to exist which were of practical advantage to the creature concerned. Into this category fall the Skiapodes, an extraordinary tribe of the Libyan Desert. These creatures were said to have only one foot, which was so enormous that when the sun was at its hottest they could lie down on their backs and raise the foot like a huge umbrella above their heads to keep off the powerful rays. The name skiapodes actually means 'shade-foot'. Despite having only one leg they could apparently hop from place to place with great agility and amazing speed.

Equally well equipped to ward off the harmful effects of the hot sun is a race with huge lower lips, which possessed incredible elasticity. When these extraordinary people lay down to sleep, the lip could be stretched over their entire faces to shade them from the burning rays. Living in Scythia, according to Bartholomeus Anglicus, was a race of men who customarily remained nude, but could neverthe-less both preserve their modesty and keep out the draughts with the aid of their own ears, which were knee-length and could be closely swathed around their bodies like a cloak.

Incredible though these alleged natural deformities may seem, they are no more so than the self-inflicted malforma-tions still found in some parts of the world. Some tribes in Africa do actually distort their own lips until they are as large as plates by the regular insertion of discs of increasing size in the pursuit of some strange concept of human beauty. The so-called 'giraffe-women' who stretch their own necks with collar-like bands are another example, while the habit of binding baby girls' feet, as in China, died hard despite its obvious crippling effects and vigorous attempts at educating the population.

Strange sexual practices and weird abnormalities were sometimes reported among subhuman races. Pliny says that according to the Greek historian Duvis, there existed races in India among whom it was common practice to have sexual intercourse with beasts. The offspring which were conceived as a result of such bestial acts of lust were said to be half human, half animal. The kinds of creatures which participated in these displays of bestiality are not specified.

A hermaphroditic subhuman race called the Androgyni is described by Pliny. Each individual is said to have the entire reproductive systems of both sexes. The left breast is that of a man, the right that of a woman. They are said to be capable of adopting either the male or female role in copulation, and to be able to beget or conceive according to the nature of their participation. Sir Thomas Browne reminds us, however, that 'Hermaphrodites although they include the parts of both sexes, and may be sufficiently potent in either; yet unto a conception require a separated sex, and cannot impregnate themselves'.

Both Odoric and Sir John Mandeville report the distressing effects of extreme heat on the male genital organs. In climates like that of certain parts of Ethiopia, men's testicles were reported to hang down to their knees, with excruciatingly painful and no doubt embarrassing results. Fortunately it was possible to combat these difficulties with the liberal application of cooling ointments. The following description of what happened on the island of Trinor occurs in *Mandeville's Travels*: 'That eche Yle is so hot that thour the grete hete of the eyr that manys privite hangith doun to here kneis that dwellyn ther. But the men of that contre that knowe the kynde of here lond vsyn colde medecynys and onymentis, that restreyneth it thour remedye for swich myschef and for gret vnese that fallyth among hem.'

Mandeville notes a custom among both men and women in Ethiopia of lying naked and totally immersed in water throughout the hottest part of the day in order to counteract the ill effect of the climate. Marco Polo also records this detail.

Strange creatures like those mentioned in this chapter could not, of course, be brought back as proof of their existence, and it is perhaps surprising that such exhibits were not demanded before any credence was placed in stories of this kind. A clue is furnished in the accounts of a peculiar race of people with eight fingers or toes on each hand or foot. In this instance it is alleged that these beasts died immediately they were withdrawn from their own native climate, and it is not difficult to see that fabricators of extra-ordinary stories were usually able to create plausible excuses with the aid of their own powers of invention.

CHAPTER FIVE
Sex and Bawdy

ACCORDING TO various classical authorities, camels couple back to back and spend all day in the act of mating. The male camel, whose penis is so sinewy that it used to be considered ideal for the manufacture of bow-strings, was exceedingly fierce if interrupted during copulation, and on such occasions nobody but the keeper would dare go near it.

The camel is only one of a long list of animals stated to copulate back to back. Stories of this quirk of animal behaviour can be traced back as far as the fourth century B.C. and were once in common circulation. Among others regularly noted for this practice are the lion, tiger, hare, panther, lynx, hyena, elephant and rhinoceros. The criterion was that the method of coition was linked to the method of urination, those animals which urinate rearwards also practising retrocopulation. It has also been suggested that those who adopt back-to-back copulation do so from an excess of natural delicacy.

One such modest creature, the elephant, was exceptionally slow to sexual arousal. It can therefore readily be imagined that elephants never committed adultery, having absolutely no inclination for it. Similarly, fighting among the bulls over the cows of the herd was totally alien to their nature. The bestiaries tell us that without some form of powerful external stimulant they were unable to copulate at all. If a pair of elephants wished to conceive, they had to journey eastwards towards Eden, where the female plucked the fruit of the mandrake, ate some of it herself and then offered the remainder to the male.

Strange superstitions had surrounded the mandrake from the earliest times. A member of the potato family, it had a very thick root, often forked, and bore a crude resemblance to the human form. Sometimes people actually increased this likeness by fashioning it with a knife. According to popular belief the mandrake uttered an eerie shriek if pulled from the ground, and anyone who heard it would die. Besides having narcotic properties, the mandrake was highly regarded as a remedy for sterility and was considered to be a potent aphrodisiac for men and beasts alike. People thought it sprang spontaneously from human sperm that had overflowed upon the ground.

With the aid of this root the elephants were able not only to copulate satisfactorily but also to conceive. The gestation period for elephants was once thought to be ten years but, perhaps fortunately for the female elephant, this proved to be false, and Pliny points out correctly that it is in fact only two years. When about to go into labour, the cow elephant was said to wade out into a lake or river until the water came up to her udders, and there to give birth, with the bull standing guard on the shore to preserve both the cow and the calf from the attacks of their traditional enemy the serpent.

Not everybody believed that the elephant was totally indifferent to sex. In some countries men played upon their lecherous instincts to lure them to an untimely end. Bartholomew Anglicus gives the following account of a ruse which could be used to catch them:

Among the Ethiopians in some countries elephants be hunted in this wise: there go into the desert two maidens all naked and bare, with open hair of the head: and one of them beareth a vessel, and the other a sword. And these maidens begin to sing alone: and the beast hath liking when he heareth their song, and liketh their teats, and falleth asleep anon for liking of the song, and then the one maid striketh him in the throat with a sword, and the other taketh his blood in a vessel, and with that blood the people of the same country dye cloth, and done colour it therewith.

Nor was everyone agreed that elephants use the rear-ward method of presentment in intercourse. Instead some people maintained that they adopt the usual posture for quadrupeds, for they felt it was quite impossible for two such huge, clumsy brutes to perform this delicate little manœuvre to their mutual satisfaction in this strange back-to-back position. Nevertheless the great weight of the male was thought to present something of a problem, and those authorities who adopted this view usually also asserted that the male mounted the female by floating above her on a lake during coition, so that the buoyancy of the water could prevent her from being squashed. A commonly accepted alternative was for the male to dig a pit for the female to lie in during copulation, while he balanced himself precariously above her on the rim.

In complete contrast to the elephant, the lion was thought to possess an exceptionally passionate nature, and as a consequence to be excessively jealous of the female. Such was their sensuality and the violence of their instincts that they coupled indiscriminately with other feline animals, but the adulterous lioness who cuckolded her mate by indulging her sexual appetite with a leopard was inevitably betrayed by his odour unless she took steps to hide it. If her mate found out that he had been betrayed in this way he would devote all his energy to punishing her. To avoid these reprisals she would accordingly wash away the tell-tale odour by bathing herself in a stream after inter-course.

Like other varieties with sharp claws the lioness was believed to bear cubs only once in her lifetime, for the scratching by the young ones impatient to be born would damage the walls of the womb so severely that she was unable to conceive again. By a curious paradox, although these cubs were believed capable of causing such damage to the womb by their activities before birth, the bestiarists claimed that they were born lifeless, and that they remained so unless the father breathed vitality into them on the third day.

Alternative positions for intercourse are discussed by Sir Thomas Browne in his book *Pseudodoxia Epidemica*, or,

Enquiries into very many Received and Commonly Presumed Truths (1646) : *

Nor is there one, but many ways of Coition, according to divers shapes and different conformations. For some couple laterally or sidewise as wormes; some circularly or by complication as Serpents; some pronely, that is by contraction of prone parts in both, as Apes, Porcupines, Hedgehogges, and such as are termed Mollia, as the Cuttle-fish and the Purple; some mixtly, that is, the male ascending the female, or by application of the prone parts of one unto the postick parts of the other, as most quadrupeds; some aversely, as all Crustaceous Animals, Lobsters, Shrimps and Crevises, and also Retromingents, as Panthers, Tigers and Hares. This is the constant Law of their Coition, this they observe and transgress not.

Of man's practice in regard to sex Browne is sharply critical, hinting darkly at sodomy, intercourse with beasts and other promiscuous activities. Yet it is apparent from the following paragraph that it is not the activities themselves which disturb him most but the fact that they are practised openly and without shame:

Only the Vitiosity of man hath acted the varieties thereof —not content with a digression from sex or species, hath in his own kind run through the Anomolies of venery, and been so bold, not only to act, but represent to view, the Irregular ways of lust.

Some creatures were regarded as particularly lustful. The goat was one such animal, the male being said to practise coition when no more than seven days old. Both males and females bred better without horns, so that these were often removed. She-goats were particularly hot in coupling, yet there was a perfectly simple explanation, according to Pliny. Instead of breathing through their nostrils like other animals, they breathed permanently through their ears, remaining consequently in a persistently feverish condition. This they presumably relieved by continual sexual activity.

The sex of kids was said by Aristotle to depend largely on the direction of the wind, females being produced more

* Hereafter called *Vulgar Errors*.

plentifully when the wind blew from the south and males when it proceeded from the north. In the case of rams an entirely different factor governed the sex of the offspring, a ligature being placed on the left testicle if males were required, and on the right testicle if females were preferred.

Also specially noted for their lecherous behaviour were cats. The female allowed the male no peace at all, but constantly incited it to coition, caterwauling almost non-stop in the process. Of the tom cat Bartholomew Anglicus reports that he is 'a full lecherous beast in youth, swift, and merry, and leapeth and reseth on everything that is to fore him. . . . In time of love is hard fighting for wives, and one scratcheth and rendeth the other grievously with biting and with claws. And he maketh a ruthful noise and a ghastful, when one proffereth to fight with another. . . '.

The most lustful of all female animals, however, was the mare. 'In fact,' declared Aristotle, 'the mare is said to go a-horsing; and the term derived from the habits of this one animal serves as a term of abuse applicable to such females of the human species as are unbridled in the way of sexual appetite.'

Belief in the immoderate lechery of the mare persisted into the Middle Ages, as a thirteenth-century book called *The Ancrene Riwle* (Guide for Anchoresses) proves. 'Confession must be naked,' the unknown author writes, meaning, of course, not that a woman should go to her father confessor without any clothes on but that she should be absolutely specific about the sin which she has committed. '"Sir," a woman will say, "I have had a lover," or she will say, "I have been foolish about myself." This is not naked confession. Do not wrap it up. Take off the trimmings. Make yourself clear and say: "Sir, God's mercy! I am a foul stud mare, a stinking whore."' *

Though mares were positively indecent in their sexuality, offering themselves shamelessly to any stallion who happened to be handy, horses were thought by contrast to possess a very strong sense of moral propriety and to be filled with delicate sensibility. It was apparently this innate

---

* Rendered into modern English by M. B. Salu, London, 1955.

sense of moral decency which drove one stallion to extremes. Unfortunately the poor beast, having coupled with
a mare somewhat older than himself, discovered to his
shame and horror that she was none other than his own
dam. The shock of this dreadful revelation was more than
he could bear and, according to Pliny, in a fit of distraction
he committed suicide by hurling himself over a cliff.

Because they showed exceptional strength, which made
them invaluable in agricultural work, mules were highly
sought after, and mares were therefore encouraged to mate
with asses in order to produce them. Unless they themselves
had been suckled by females of the same genus as the
stallion, however, mares of either species were adamant in
refusing to copulate with the stallions of the other. Farmers
therefore considered it a good idea to take foals away from
their own dams under cover of darkness and put them to the
udders of a mare or she-ass as appropriate.

Some female creatures were the victims of such overwhelming sexual passions that they could conceive without
intercourse with the male. A beast which fell into this category was the female partridge, notorious for her concu-
piscence. Just standing face to face with the cock bird or
sniffing its odour was quite enough to bring on a pregnancy. Simply putting out her own tongue was sufficient to
produce an orgasm, while hearing the voice of the male
from far off would result in conception.

No doubt the countryside would have been quickly over-
run with these birds had not the activities of the male
partridges played an important part in preventing the pro-
liferation of the species. For the females were not alone in
their addiction to sexual venery, and the excessive lust of the
male birds would often drive them to break the eggs of
the female, for fear that having to sit upon them would deter
her from intercourse. Though they were quickly exhausted
by their own sexual excesses, the nature of their desires was
such that the cocks were forever fighting each other over
the hens. It was considered the privilege of the victor to
compel his rival to submit to sodomy, and this he inevitably
did without complaint.

Men used to believe that vultures had no desire to copulate, and accordingly never indulged in sexual commerce. Intercourse was thought totally unnecessary for the procreation of chicks in this species, the females being able in some unexplained fashion to impregnate themselves without the intervention of the male. This fallacy was offered by the bestiarists as a reproach to those men who did not believe that the Virgin Mary was as chaste as the Bible stories would indicate. Birds were not the only warm-blooded creatures believed to be able to impregnate themselves without male assistance. Pliny tells us that mice, which are exceptionally prolific, could induce a pregnancy by licking salt. Women too could conceive without the help of men, so that a salt-free diet might have its advantages.

Excessive lust is not of course an exclusively female characteristic. The male snake, for instance, was said to be much addicted to sexual venery. Urged on by desires which could not be met adequately in its relationship with its own natural mate, it would leave her side and go away by itself to call aloud to the female eel and summon it from the depths of the ocean to meet its embraces. On her approach it would obligingly vomit its venom at the water's edge in order to avoid poisoning her during cotion. After they had enjoyed their unnatural pleasures to their mutual satisfaction, they would part, the snake swallowing its venom again before returning to its own mate.

The accounts of the union of these two animals gave the bestiarists a wonderful opportunity to discourse at length on adulterous relationships between human beings, and they took full advantage of it, offering admonitions as they felt appropriate. Yet somewhat unfairly, though the husband is warned against seeking his pleasures outside the confines of the marital bed, it is the wife who comes in for most of the criticism. If her husband had strayed, it was regarded as principally her own fault for having failed to accept his conjugal embraces willingly and cheerfully, and for having driven him by her own shortcomings into the waiting arms of other women.

The stag too was an immoderately salacious animal, and its

penis was so rigid that the hind would submit to intercourse only under compulsion. Its unparalleled excesses of sexual venery were believed to shorten its life considerably, 'for castrated animals in every species are longer lived than they which retain their virilities'.

Towards the end of the rutting season, when the stag had over-indulged in sexual activity, its penis was thought to wither and drop off. Although this loss was thought to be directly related to excessive sex there is no indication that men feared the same results from their own immoderation, or in any way restrained their activities on this account. In any event the stag was inconvenienced only by a temporary incapacity, for by the next season it would have grown a new yard and could resume its customary sexual pursuits.

Sit Thomas Browne denies that there was any truth in these stories. His reservation about the theory that the penis could drop off was based on the fact that stags which had fallen to the hunter were always fully equipped for a normal sex life. The idea that stags could grow another penis was discounted on the grounds that the organs associated with procreation were incapable of growing again. This is explained in his own words:

> Now the ground hereof was surely the observation of this part in deer after immoderate venery, and about the end of their Rut, which sometimes becomes so relaxed and pendulous, it cannot be quite retracted: and being often beset with flies, it is conceived to rot, and at last to fall from the body. . . . And reason will also correct us: for spermatical parts, or such as are framed from the seminal principles of parents, although homogeneous or similarly, will not admit a Regeneration, much less will they receive an integral restauration. . . .

Involuntary self-castration was said to take place among boars, who were afflicted in their early years by an unbearable irritation in the genital region. This they attempted to relieve by rubbing themselves against the bark of trees, a practice which had disastrous results. Deliberate self-castration by biting off its own testicles was, however, said to be practised by beavers when hunted (Plate 16). This animal was much prized for the secretion of its genitals, which was known as beaver oil and thought to have special medicinal properties. An account of the circumstances is given in the bestiaries:

Accordingly, Physiologus reports, that when he finds himself pursued by the huntsman, he bites off his own testicles and casts them down in the path of the hunter, then escapes by flight. Furthermore, if he is followed by a second huntsman, he raises himself up and displays his private parts to him. And the latter, observing the absence of the testicles, abandons his pursuit.

It has been pointed out, however, that self-castration in this fashion would be impossible for the beaver, since the real testicles are located internally. Other protuberances are instead mistaken for these organs, as Sir Thomas Browne, that invaluable commentator on sexual matters, explains:

For these Cods or Follicles are found in both Sexes, though somewhat more protuberant in the male. There is hereto no derivation of the seminal parts, nor any passage from hence, unto the Vessels of Ejaculation: some perforations onely in the part itself, through which the humour included doth exudate: as may be observed in such as are fresh, and not much dried with age.

A lustful beast said to castrate its own male young was the onager, or wild ass. This animal was believed to possess such a compelling appetite for sexual indulgences that it was unable to countenance possible future rivalry, even from its own male young. To some extent the beast only defeated its own object by behaving in this way, for in order to protect her offspring from mutilation by the father, the female would withdraw from the society of her mate until the foal was able to defend itself from attacks of this kind.

The female hyena apparently had the ability to induce its own pregnancies without assistance from the male. The way in which it achieved this feat is not actually specified. In addition men thought that it changed its sex from year to year, and for these reasons the hyena was looked upon as a particularly disgusting beast. The conception of the annual sex change was not, however, universally held. By seventeenth-century standards the male was regarded as a superior being to the female, and whereas it was considered to be within the bounds of reason that a creature could convert from a female to a male, the reverse process of changing from the male to the female, that is from perfection to imperfection, was contrary to the laws of nature, and therefore clearly unthinkable.

Nowadays the reproductive system of hares is considered so typical of the processes of mammals in general that it is used as an everyday example in the schoolroom. It is therefore difficult to understand why the sex of this small animal was a mystery which puzzled mankind down the ages. Various theories were held about the range of its sexual organs and the exact nature of their functions. The only fact which emerges beyond all possible dispute, however, is that there existed a large body of opinion which attributed to this animal some kind of sexual abnormality.

Plutarch was one of those who believed that each hare possessed the complete reproductive system of both male and female. Some adherents to this explanation also saw in this a special gift of providence to mankind, for because of their ability to adopt either the active or the passive role in coition, they were able to reproduce with greater rapidity. Man benefited from this special facility because hares were regarded as a great delicacy in some societies, and were available in greater abundance for the table.

When this kind of conjunction of both sexes in one animal occurred, Aristotle nevertheless maintained that a state of constant impotence existed in the organs relating to one of the sexes, so that it could not copulate freely as either male or female by turns. Most experts were moreover agreed that among hermaphroditic creatures two separate animals were required, one to fulfil each sexual role, before offspring could be produced. An alternative notion was that, on reaching maturity, such creatures automatically selected one sex and indulged it to the total exclusion of the other, rigidly enforcing a sort of virgin state on that sex which it rejected.

Two other popular theories were either that the hare

experienced a transexion at established intervals, or underwent a sex mutation at some time during its existence. The conception of a sex change was not intrinsically unacceptable, for human beings were known to have changed sex, though it was thought that those who had done so were those who had mistakenly been classified as women at birth yet had ultimately revealed themselves to the world as men. The intellectual objection to the theory of periodic transexion was as already explained in relation to the hyena, that is that 'degenerous effemination', or a decline from the indisputable perfection of the male to the imperfection of the female, was totally irrational and therefore contrary to the laws of nature. The idea of a single sex mutation during its lifetime was not intrinsically unacceptable, however, provided that the change was from the female to the male, and not the other way round.

Delving into the reasons for the almost universally held fallacies about the sex of hares, Sir Thomas Browne draws various interesting conclusions. He states that like the beaver, hares of both sexes contain 'a double bag or Tumour in the groin, commonly called the Cod or Castor'. These were mistaken for the testicles, and led to the false belief that females possessed male organs. Similarly, cavities observed in the male were wrongly identified as the female orifice.

A graphic account of the final phase of the argument is found in *Vulgar Errors*:

The last foundation was Retromingency or pissing backward; for men observing both sexes to urine backward, or aversely between their legs, they might conceive there was a foeminine part in both; wherein they are deceived by ignorance of the just and proper site of the Pizzel, or part designed unto the Excretion of urine; which in the hare holds not the common position, but is aversely seated, and in its distention enclines unto the Coccix or Scut. Now from the nature of this position, there ensueth a necessity of Retrocopulation, which also promoteth the conceit: for some observing them to couple without ascension, have not been able to judge of male or female, or to determine the proper sex in either.

Also accredited to the hare was the process of superfoetation, or the fertilization of a second or even a third egg while the first is still developing in the womb. Most writers regarded this capacity as unique, but there were some who claimed that women too had this ability, and cautioned them against the policy of indulging extra-marital relationships during pregnancy: 'For the Matrix (which some have called another Animal within us, and which is not subjected unto the law of our will), after reception of its proper Tenant, may yet receive a strange and spurious inmate.'

Lack of advanced scientific equipment and modern techniques was a very great handicap to our ancestors, for without them they were unable to organize the minute observation and documentation of animal behaviour which are possible for scientists of our own era. Exactly how life originally began is a mystery which still torments us, yet until quite recent times the method by which life was simply handed on from one generation to the next was in the case of certain animals an equally great riddle.

Confronted by minute animal life whose origin was unknown, men evolved a theory that in some miraculous way creatures like maggots and eels could just spring to life of their own accord from inorganic or decaying matter. Aristotle in his *Generation of Animals* explains this generally accepted notion as follows:

So with animals, some spring from parent animals according to their kind, whilst others grow spontaneously and not from kindred stock; and of these instances of spontaneous generation some come from putrefying earth or vegetable matter, as is the case with a number of insects, while others are spontaneously generated in the inside of animals out of the secretions of their several organs.

Each of the various species engendered in this fashion was thought to spring from certain identifiable substances. Some insects, for instance, were thought to grow from dew on leaves or flowers, and others from the decomposing flesh of animals. Virgil claims both these origins for bees in his *Georgics*. First he gives us a beautiful account of the way in which bees were normally conceived:

Most you shall marvel at this habit peculiar to bees—
That they have no sexual union: their bodies never
                      dissolve
Lax into love, nor bear with pangs of birth their young.
But all by themselves from leaves and sweet herbs they
                   will gather
Their children in their mouths. . . .*

Alternatively he explains how they may be generated from putrid carcasses of cattle:

. . . from the oxen's bellies all over their rotting flesh
Creatures are humming, swarming through the
                   wreckage of their ribs—
Huge and trailing clouds of bees, that now in the
                    treetops
Unite and hang like a bunch of grapes from the pliant
                   branches.†

Snakes were thought to grow of their own free will from the spinal marrow of dead men, though certain writers alleged that this could happen only in the corpses of men who had led immoral lives. John Lyly, however, held a different view about the origin of snakes and claimed that they were 'engendered by the breath of the huge elephant'.

The offspring of creatures resulting from this process of spontaneous generation were regarded by Aristotle as inevitably corrupt. They differed completely from their parents, not only in appearance but also in habit. They were, moreover, incapable of reproducing themselves, either in their own form or that of their parents.

These ancient beliefs may seem to us incredibly naïve, yet we have to bear in mind that this belief in the spontaneous generation of animals was an immensely popular one which was still widely postulated even as late as the nineteenth century. It was in fact not until a century ago that the famous scientist Louis Pasteur conducted a series of experiments in which he finally proved conclusively that it was quite impossible for life to spring from dead or inorganic matter that was truly sterile. In this way he successfully demolished

* Book IV, ll. 197–201.
† Book IV, ll. 554–7.

a notion which had been regarded as an established scientific fact for many hundreds of years.

Before leaving the subject of spontaneous generation, we must consider two very curious phenomena which really captured the imaginations of the credulous. These were tree geese and barnacle geese, sometimes confused in literature, but which actually represented two quite separate developments of the same basic legend.

So far as it can be established, the idea of the tree geese and barnacle geese (commonly referred to as bernekke) first started in Ireland and Scotland, where these birds were thought to abound. The tree goose, which is both described and also illustrated in Gerard's *Herbal*, was said to spring from the fruit of trees growing on the sea-shore. As it grew ripe the fruit would fall into the water, and on contact with the brine would immediately turn into a goose.

In the twelfth century both Alexander Neckam in his book *De naturis rerum* and Giraldus Cambrensis in *Topography of Ireland* describe these geese. The account given by Giraldus reads as follows:

> They resemble the marsh-geese, but are smaller. Being at first gummy excrescences from pine-beams floating on the waters, and then enclosed in shells to secure their free growth, they hang up by their beaks, like seaweed attached to timber. Being in the process of time well covered with feathers, they either fall into the water or take their flight in the free air, their nourishment and growth being supplied, while they are bred in this very unaccountable manner, from the juices of the wood in the sea-water. I have often seen with my own eyes more than a thousand minute embryos of birds of this species on the seashore, hanging from one piece of timber, covered with shells, and already formed. No eggs are laid by these birds after copulation, as is the case with birds in general; the hen never sits on eggs in order to hatch them; in no corner of the world are they seen either to pair or build nests.

Whether these legends arose out of a genuine attempt to explain the origin of these birds which, being migratory, were never seen to breed in the countries where these legends circulated, or whether they were a deliberate fabrication by those who were not over scrupulous in matters of religious observance in order to mislead their more conscientious friends, is not established. Nevertheless because they sprang to life of their own free will and not as a result of sexual intercourse, these birds were regarded by some as an acceptable and no doubt welcome change of diet during the Lenten season.

Giraldus tells us that in some parts of Ireland religious men from the bishop down had no qualms about eating these birds on fast days. This he considered both illogical and a serious error. For Adam was not conceived by sexual intercourse, 'yet if anyone had eaten the thigh of our first parent, which was really flesh, although not born of flesh, I should think him not guiltless of having eaten flesh'.

Sexual intercourse as a means of its begetting was, then, a major objection to meat as an item of diet. This is another reflection of the widespread religious belief that whereas matrimony was preferable to promiscuity, and copulation essential for the continuance of the human race, celibacy was to be regarded as a higher state than carnal incontinence.

There was in addition a school of thought which favoured the view that indulgence in sex shortened life. Sir Thomas Browne upheld this view, but tried to place it in a better perspective, remarking that intercourse was:

Certainly a confessed and undeniable enemy to longaevity, and not only as a sign in the complexional desire and impetuosity, but also as a cause in the frequent act, or iterated performance thereof. For though we consent not with that Philosopher, who thinks a spermatical emission unto the weight of one drachm, is aequivalent unto the effusion of sixty ounces of bloud; yet considering the exolution and languor ensuing that act in some, the extenuation and marcour in others, and the visible acceleration it maketh of age in most; we cannot but think it much abridgeth our days.

From this it would appear that our ancestors were faced with a choice of following a prolonged and celibate life or enjoying a short but sexually active one. Fortunately for their descendants it appears that many of them elected the latter.

CHAPTER SIX

Beastly Behaviour

THE BONNACON, when hotly pursued by the hunter, emits an enormous fart so foul that its attackers are forced to retire in confusion. Any trees or shrubs which happen to be in the way of this violent and disgusting blast burst instantly into flames.

Or so, at least, the bestiarists maintained, and there may indeed be some substance in this, for some animals are known to evacuate the bowels when in flight. In the judgment of the bestiary writers, the bonnacon's nauseating prowess was a special benefit conferred upon it by nature. It compensated the beast, better known to the modern reader as the bison, for the uselessness of its horns, which were curved in such a way that they could not be used as a defensive weapon. When it performed this feat, it simultaneously discharged the entire contents of its bowel in the faces of its attackers, and the quantity was sufficient to cover three whole acres of ground. In this way, the medieval writers claimed, the animal made up for the deficiencies of its front end by the peculiar potency of its rear.

Medieval limners who were responsible for illustrating the bestiaries naturally wished to portray the beast in the midst of this characteristic act, and the modern reader who wonders how this could possibly be depicted will find an example in Plate 17. In the original the fart is painted blue.

While the bonnacon repelled with a fart, the panther attracted with a belch. For when the panther has eaten his fill, he falls into a deep sleep which lasts for three whole days. On awaking, he emits a loud belch, which smells so sweet that it draws all animals after him. His voice sounds like a bell, and though his head is so terrifying that he has to hide it, the colours of his body are diverse and beautiful, so that other beasts cannot help being hypnotized by them. In this way the panther is able to lure his prey. The only animal that is afraid of the panther is the dragon, which flees at once to its den when it hears his voice, for it cannot bear the smell of the panther's breath, knowing that it is poisonous.

The true panther, say the bestiarists, is Jesus Christ, who attracts all men to his side even from the ends of the earth. He descends into Hell and shackles the Great Dragon, who of course represents the Devil. Then on the third day he rises from his sleep and emits a belch, which draws all men to him by its sweet odour.

The modern reader cannot help feeling puzzled at the freedom of these references in religious works to those two socially unacceptable emissions, the fart and the belch. Even the terms themselves are normally considered too coarse for polite conversation, yet there are no workable alternatives that can be substituted, the subjects being considered simply unfit for discussion.

More surprising still is the identification of the panther with Jesus Christ, for the image of Christ belching would on the face of it seem irreverent in the extreme. Yet it has to be remembered that belching is not considered a lapse of social etiquette in every society. Indeed in some it is regarded as not only acceptable but more or less obligatory as a gesture of politeness. Even today in certain countries in the Far East a resounding belch is regarded not as a breach of good manners but as a proper indication of the enjoyment of a good meal. It is customary in such countries for guests at a dinner party to offer loud and appreciative belches as a compliment to the hostess.

The books in which these comparisons between Christ and the panther were drawn were prepared in a spirit of piety and religious fervour and it is clear from the context that no disrespect is intended. These bestiary writings, though condemned by a few, were generally accepted by the majority as authoritative religious handbooks, containing a wealth of teaching on moral and Christian attitudes. What appears there was written down by serious-minded men whose only object was to discover the truth and record it for the enlightenment of others. The truth which they sought so earnestly was not biological, but the moral and religious truth which God exhibited for the benefit of mankind in the countless examples of nature.

There is evidence, however, that these breaches of the socially accepted standards of behaviour were discussed with relative freedom in the Middle Ages. Chaucer certainly had no scruples about referring to them when it suited his literary purposes. In 'The Reeve's Tale' for instance, two poor students spend a night under the miller's roof, sharing the only bedroom with the entire family. Chaucer describes what happens when the miller and his wife retire to bed:

> The miller had taken so much booze unheeded
> He snorted like a cart-horse in his sleep
> And vented other noises, loud and deep.
> His wife joined in the chorus hot and strong;
> Two furlongs off you might have heard their song.*

And in 'The Miller's Tale' he tells us what happens to Absalon the clerk when he mounts to Alison's bedroom window by night with the help of a ladder, not knowing that she is already entertaining another lover, Nicholas, in her bed-chamber:

> Now Nicholas had risen for a piss,
> And thought he could improve upon the jape
> And make him kiss his arse ere he escape,
> And opening the window with a jerk,
> Stuck out his arse, a handsome piece of work,
> Buttocks and all, as far as to the haunch.
> Said Absalon, all set to make a launch,
> 'Speak, pretty bird, I know not where thou art!'
> This Nicholas at once let fly a fart
> As loud as if it were a thunder-clap.
> He was near blinded by the blast, poor chap. . . .'†

Nor was Chaucer the only courtly poet who introduced

* *The Canterbury Tales*, translated by Nevill Coghill.
† ibid.

such matters into his work. At the same time as he was working on *The Canterbury Tales*, that is, in the final quarter of the fourteenth century, another great writer whose real identity has never been positively established was composing *The Vision of Piers the Plowman*. In a lively tavern scene he describes Glutton drinking his ale in company with such lusty characters as Hick the Hackneyman, Clement the Cobler, and Clarice the Whore of Cock Lane, the notorious London street to which prostitutes were conducted after they had been pilloried:

By that time Glutton had put down more than a gallon of ale, and his guts were beginning to rumble like a couple of greedy sows. Then before you had time to say the Our Father, he had pissed a couple of quarts and blown such a blast on the round horn of his rump that all who heard it had to hold their noses and wished to God he would plug it with a bunch of gorse.

These extracts, though directed at a universal audience, portray scenes of low life exhibited for comic purposes. The passage from *Piers Plowman* has a didactic function, despite the unashamedly bawdy presentation, and is meant to indicate the folly of vice in order to teach people to look for a different way of life. The accounts in the bestiaries are offered in an absolutely serious vein, their object being not to titillate but to instruct, and the writer's attitude is one of simple acceptance of the various functions of the body.

It is interesting to consider what did, in fact, disgust our ancestors in an age when references to the fart and the belch could be freely offered, not only by courtly writers but also by religious ones. The examples quoted from the bestiaries, where these matters were discussed without either embarrassment or abhorrence, and from *The Vision of Piers the Plowman* and *The Canterbury Tales*, make it clear that the distinction drawn is partly a matter of literary treatment and partly of the way in which these natural functions are carried out.

Medieval man could accept without disgust the fact of the bonnacon evacuating its bowel in the faces of its pursuers because nature had provided this miraculous means of defence where no other existed. What he could not stomach was the popular belief that the owl fouled its own nest and sat in excrement up to the chin, for this was simply a dirty and therefore obnoxious habit. For rather surprisingly, despite the primitive methods of sanitation and the general lack of knowledge about the connection between dirt and disease, great store was placed on cleanliness and personal hygiene in the Middle Ages. A famous anonymous poem of the fourteenth century entitled 'Cleanness' extols this very virtue, which was symbolically associated with purity of the soul.

According to a heated debate between two birds in *The Owl and the Nightingale*, written in the thirteenth century and, like so many other writings of the period, anonymous, the owl's habit of defiling its own nest made it an object of disgust to men and birds alike. It was in addition feared and hated because it flew only by night and augured misfortune and death.

All creatures which brought physical danger to human beings were in fact looked on with fear and horror. The hoopoe came within this category, for it was believed to desecrate human graves and feed on the contents. In addition it consumed dung and lined its nest with human excrement, or at least so the bestiarists believed. Any man tainted with the blood of this fowl when retiring for the night was certain to be pursued by nightmares of being strangled by the devil.

Though held in such high esteem by the ancient Egyptians that it was classed as a sacred bird, the ibis was in general regarded as a rather disgusting creature on account of its habit of purging itself by inserting its long, thin beak into its own fundament. Its adherence to a diet consisting almost exclusively of snakes was held in great abhorrence, for eating snakes would have been considered fatal to human beings, and its giving birth to serpents through concentrating on this form of food, as the bestiarists claimed, was thought to be a fate no worse than it deserved.

Revolting external appearances could also disgust medieval man, particularly where the rear end of the animal was concerned. Monkeys were heartily disliked for this reason. One bestiary account may be translated as follows: 'Indeed the whole body of the monkey is abominable; yet their backsides are disgusting and loathsome in the extreme. The Devil in the same way had a sound base in heaven among the angels, yet he was a sly hypocrite within and lost his tail as an indication that he would perish utterly in the end.'

This reaction is perhaps hardly surprising, for even today the sight of some of the occupants of the monkey house at the Zoo is sufficient to raise a guffaw among many of the onlookers. A few years ago a society sprang up in America which succeeded in raising a substantial sum of money for the sole purpose of putting knickers on cows. No doubt this idea would have recommended itself to many people in the Middle Ages, but it would appear that nobody thought of it, either in relation to cows or monkeys.

Sex was another subject which could arouse disgust in the medieval mind, but it was nevertheless regarded with a great deal of curiosity, and its constant recurrence in animal lore is a reflection of this interest.

It is perhaps hardly surprising that doubts arose as to the morality of sexual relationships under the influence of the Christian religion, which emphasized heavily the celibacy of Christ's life, and his conception by a pure virgin. Although he was begotten by God the Father on the Virgin Mary, there was no physical union in the normal sense. In multitheistic religions the gods often begat children on human women, but almost always this resulted from a carnal relationship in which the god either raped the object of his lust or enjoyed normal sexual intercourse freely offered. Usually he came to her either in human form or in the guise of some beast noted for its lechery, such as a bull. Occasionally, however, he would sire an infant without carnal activity, as when Zeus, whose sexual exploits with countless human damsels were particularly notorious, came to Danäe in the guise of a shower of gold, but this was simply a ruse to outwit her father, who kept her so closely guarded that he could not manage the affair in any other way.

The early Christian fathers had in the Bible itself ample material to work on, and for the most part expressed the opinion that sex was unfortunately necessary for the continuance of the human race. They believed that sexual intercourse within matrimony was preferable to indiscriminate union of male and female, and sanctioned wedlock for those who could not live without sex, or who believed, like Chaucer's Wife of Bath, that 'Better it is to marry than to burn'. Nevertheless celibacy was considered to be a higher state and therefore infinitely to be preferred to a life of normal sexual activity. It was thus by no means uncommon for pagan married ladies to be relegated to the frustrating role of sister when their husbands were converted to Christianity.

Some people, however, actually believed that all sex was wrong, and felt that a miracle would, if necessary, ensure the continuance of the species, though in a society which lived in constant expectation of the coming of the Kingdom of God this was perhaps a matter of relatively small importance.

A very strong view is expressed by Giraldus Cambrensis, who writes: 'Blush, O wretched man, blush! At least recur to nature which, in confirmation of the faith of our best teaching continually produces and gives birth to certain animals, without union of male and female.'

Sir Thomas Browne attempts to put these notions into their proper perspective. He sees no fundamental objection to sex as a means of engendering the species, but he has definite scruples about frequent sexual intercourse because it was believed to shorten life, and consequently robbed man of his true intellectual potential. On the other hand he has very strong prejudices against any methods of copulation which deviate from what he considers the natural method in which the man covers the woman.

It was as sexual deviationists, therefore, that weasels were held in such great disgust in the Middle Ages. Contrary to the established rules of nature, the female was accused of actually receiving the male sperm into her own mouth, and conceiving in this way. When the young were ready to be born they were said to be delivered through the ear of the mother. This information was received in the medieval world with a shudder, and it was because of these practices that men were forbidden to eat weasels.

The viper was no less disgusting. There was, of course, no need to impose a ban on vipers as food, for all snakes were regarded as poisonous and therefore unfit to eat. But in any event its sex practices would have rendered it ineligible for consumption. For it was said that instead of adopting the normal method of coition, the male viper inserted its head into the mouth of the female, and spat the semen into it. The female would then bite his head off as he attempted to withdraw. Some authorities claimed that she did this in a moment of sexual ecstasy, while others alleged that it was because she was so enraged by his lecherous behaviour.

This method of engendering the species is similar to that claimed for dragons, and this is hardly surprising in view of the confusion which arose between these two beasts, one real and one mythical, and the development of themes about them which in many respects ran parallel.

Hyenas, like the weasel, were condemned as unfit for human food because of their filthy custom, already mentioned in chapter five, of changing sex from year to year. They were also known for two other disgusting habits. Firstly they imitated the sound of a man vomiting, in the confident expectation that someone would come along to rescue a fellow human being in distress. When the rescuer appeared, the hyena would pounce on him and kill him. Secondly they were reputed to live in crypts and vaults, to drag human corpses from coffins and devour them (Plate 23). In an era when it seemed important to mankind to preserve the human body after death in readiness for the Day of Resurrection, this habit of mutilating and devouring human bodies would have been regarded with particular abhorrence, and it is therefore hardly surprising that the hyena was looked on not only with disgust but also with loathing.

Sometimes tales of the characteristics of animals in which sex was noticeably absent were seized on by the bestiarists, who saw in them an opportunity for tacking on a sexual moral. The antelope provides a good example, and though the description of the animal evokes no distaste on the part of the reader, the moral is carefully calculated to fill him with disgust.

The horns of the antelope, which are large, saw-shaped and capable of felling trees, manage to get him into a great deal of trouble. When thirsty he drinks the water of the River Euphrates, on the banks of which he finds a bush called the Herecine. Attracted by the long, slender twigs, he begins to tease them with his antlers. While he is playing in this fashion, his antlers become hopelessly entangled so that he is unable to withdraw. After struggling for a while the beast panics and begins to bellow in a loud voice. The noise immediately attracts the attention of the hunter, who swiftly arrives on the scene and cuts off his head.

Bestiarists liken the two antlers to the Old and New Testaments, with which a man can saw off the nine sins of the flesh to which he falls such an easy victim. The vices listed are adultery and fornication, pride, envy and greed, homicide, slander, usury and drunkenness. The water of the Euphrates represents inebriety and the Herecine bush a whore. For wine and woman can deprive a man of his normal sense, and when the strumpet has ensnared him, the devil, in the person of the huntsman, will have him at his mercy.

It is interesting to find antlers cited here as the instrument of sexual entanglement, for there was a strong association between horns and sex. Horns of various animals were regarded not only as powerful aphrodisiacs but also as the symbol of cuckoldry. Sylvester, in his translation of *Du Bartas* * writes:

> The adulterous Sargus doth not only change
> Wives every day, in the deep streams; but (strange)
> As if the honey of Sea-loves delights
> Could not suffice his ranging appetites,
> Courting the Shee-goats on the grassie shore,
> Would horn their husbands that had horns before.

* *See* p. 106.

Touchstone, in *As You Like It*, is philosophical on the subject of cuckoldry, remarking: 'As horns are odious, they are necessary.'

Urination too did not always arouse disgust, and is another topic which calls for considerable comment in medieval animal lore.

Taking their basic data from Pliny, the bestiarists explain how the urine of the lynx solidifies into a precious stone called a ligurius, etymologically derived from *lync-urius*, which simply means 'lynx water'. Isidore de Seville states that the process of solidification takes seven days. One bestiary account of the twelfth century translated by T. H. White reads: 'When they have pissed the liquid, they cover it up in the sand as much as they can. They do this from a certain constitutional meanness, for fear that the piss should be useful as an ornament to the human race.' *

The manner in which the lynx took pains to hide its urine seemed to the ancient writers proof that it knew of mankind's wish to obtain it. Because the story of the ligurius or lynx water was regarded as a marvel of nature, it was not a matter of distaste to medieval man.

Just as the fart was employed as a weapon of defence by the bonnacon, so urination played the same role of a defensive mechanism in the case of the hedgehog, and as such was looked upon without abhorrence. Pliny tells us that the skins of hedgehogs were much sought after because they were widely used in the preparation of cloth, so that far from being useless to mankind as some people believed, they were essential if the human race was to derive any benefit from the soft hides of other animals. In addition, in some religious orders the hide of the hedgehog was worn next to the skin as an alternative to the hair shirt.

The hedgehog's normal method of defence, namely of rolling itself into a tiny ball protected by spines, was inadequate against the zealousness and keen ability of the human hunter, and a more drastic method was therefore required. Knowing that it was the skin for which it was so ruthlessly hunted, the hedgehog, when cornered, would

* p. 22.

urinate over its own skin thereby causing the spines to rot and fall out. Since it had a particular aversion to this method of self-poisoning, it normally reserved this remedy until driven to absolute extremes, and in fact sometimes held off for so long that capture would overtake it before it had succeeded in directing the noxious jet upon itself. If a man wished to be really scientific about hunting the hedgehog and to be certain that the skin remained intact, he would follow it around, observing it closely, until it urinated in the normal way upon the ground, and then close in and capture it.

It is hard to imagine that the hedgehog could have been very much in demand at any period in the history of mankind, yet according to Pliny severe measures had to be taken to prevent exploitation of the market in hedgehogs. 'Even here,' he writes, 'fraud has discovered a great source of profit by monopoly, nothing having been the subject of more frequent legislation by the senate, and every emperor without exception having been approached by complaints from the provinces.'

Whereas the hedgehog used urination as a mechanism of defence, another animal used it as an offensive weapon. This was a tiny creature called the lion's bane. It is not known whether this creature is fabulous, or whether the ancient writers actually had a real animal in mind but simply recorded mistaken ideas about its characteristics.

The lion's bane was said to be one of the three things capable of striking terror into the heart of that otherwise fearless beast the lion. The other two were white cockerels and the rumble of wagon wheels but, while the latter two merely frightened it, the lion's bane, despite its diminutive size, could actually kill the mighty king of the beasts. The taste alone was enough to poison the lion, which consequently hated it more than any other creature, and crushed it to death with its paw, or adopted any other method open to it short of actually biting the little beast. Meanwhile the lion's bane countered its attacks by spraying it liberally with urine, knowing that this would prove fatal to the lion.

Knowing its deadly properties, men hunted down the

lion's bane, burnt its body to fine ash and sprinkled it liberally on the skins of other animals to act as a kind of bait for the lion, for even the ashes were sufficient to kill it. Alternatively the ash could be left on the tracks of the lion or in places which he was known to frequent.

Normally one would expect that the use of urination for offensive rather than defensive purposes would have been frowned upon, but in this instance man's great fear of the lion was an overriding consideration, and the lion's bane's peculiar prowess was consequently the object of admiration and not disgust.

Keeping watch over an animal all day to see how many times he urinated must have been a tedious and rather nauseating affair, though as part of the proper pursuit of knowledge it could be tolerated and freely discussed. For according to *Physiologus* the arrival of the equinox could be recognized by the fact that the ass urinated seven times in the day to foretell its approach, and presumably a watch must have been kept over the beast in order to maintain a statistical check. One wonders to whom this extraordinary task could have fallen. Perhaps it was to a man of science, or to an astrologer. Alternatively perhaps some humble servant or slave had to carry out this strange duty.

The urination of one creature definitely filled mankind with loathing. This was the toad, whose water, like its spittle, was thought to be highly venomous. There were, however, heated disputes about whether the toad was capable of passing water at all. As might be expected, Sir Thomas Browne could not allow such an important matter to pass without comment, and offers a detailed argument on the subject of 'whether a Toad properly pisseth, that is distinctly and separately voideth the serous excretions'. After explaining Aristotle's theory that no oviparous animal with the single exception of the tortoise is able to urinate, he explains why people obtained mistaken notions about the toad:

The ground or occasion of this expression might from hence arise, that Toads are sometimes observed to extrude or spit out a dark and liquid matter behind: which we have

observed to be true, and a venomous condition there may be
perhaps therein, but some doubt there may be, whether this
is to be called their urine: not because it is emitted aversely
or backward, by both sexes, but because it is confounded
with the intestinal excretions and egestions of the belly:
and this way is ordinarily observed, although possible it is
that the liquid excretion may sometimes be extruded without
the other.

Of particular interest to the bestiary writers were those
animals whose characteristics resembled those of human
beings. Bears, for instance, were said to resemble people
more than any other animal in their method of copulation,
lying together in a close embrace with the male covering the
female. Of course this so-called resemblance presupposes
that humans always enjoy intercourse in the popular
'European' position, and it is possibly an indication that
this was the regular posture in the Middle Ages, just as it is
today. To what extent men and women adopted other
stances is not indicated, but Sir Thomas Browne certainly
objected to intercourse in other positions on moral and
religious grounds, considering them contrary to the laws of
nature. Yet that they did take up other postures for the sake
of expediency is obvious if we can accept the commonly
circulated story that Sir Walter Raleigh had intercourse with
a lady in waiting while standing upright against an oak.
Similarly it would seem that less inhibited individuals than
Sir Thomas Browne felt free to vary their sexual techniques
for the sake of greater enjoyment in marriage. In John
Marston's play *The Insatiate Countesse*, written between 1608
and 1613, Abigall discusses with her best friend the nature
of her relationship with her husband: 'Ile be sworne, wench,
I am of as pliant and yeelding body to him, e'en which way
hee will, hee may turne mee as hee list himselfe.'

When the female bear had conceived, she retired to the
back of the cave where, after a short pregnancy, she gave
birth to a shapeless foetus. After days of patient caressing
with her tongue the mother bear eventually succeeded in
licking her cub into shape. The expression 'to lick into
shape' which derives from this old belief is still current,

although we have forgotten its origin in the story of the bear and her cub.

Stories of exceptional maternal devotion were related about certain animals and because these could be compared with human experience they too were of special interest. One of these concerned the tigress, who was passionately attached to her offspring. Hunters, knowing her temperament, realized that if they stole a cub they would be relentlessly pursued by the mother, who would stop at nothing to get back her cub. They therefore prepared themselves for this eventuality by taking with them a supply of mirrors or glass balls, and when the mother, having discovered her loss, ran dangerously close, they tossed her a mirror. Seeing her own face reflected in the glass she would at first mistake it for her cub, slacken her pace and attempt to suckle it. When she discovered that she had been tricked she would resume her pursuit, whereupon the hunter would again employ the same ruse. Notwithstanding the fact that she had already been tricked in this fashion, the tigress would again be misled by the glass, which she would temporarily believe was her stolen cub. In this way the hunter would eventually manage to escape, and the cub would be lost to the unfortunate mother for ever (Plate 2).

The other, rather different, story of maternal devotion, already mentioned in Chapter Two, relates to the monkey. For it is said that when the monkey bears twins, she loves one of her offspring passionately and hates the other with equal passion. Her practice is to carry the one which she loves in her arms so that she can see its face, while the one which she scorns is relegated to her shoulders, where it rides pick-a-back out of sight. But when pursued by the hunter she eventually tires and drops the one which she loves, while the one which she detests clings to her back until they reach safety.

The pelican too was believed to be excessively devoted to its young. Yet eventually in a savage outburst of temper the parents, enraged because the fledglings flap their wings tiresomely in their faces, retaliate with such force that the young are killed. After three days the mother resuscitates them by tearing open her own breast and pouring out her lifeblood over the young ones. There are obvious parallels with the story of the crucifixion and resurrection of Christ, and needless to say the bestiary writers placed heavy emphasis on this.

There were in fact several versions of the story of the pelican, and this was only one of them, though the most popular. References to the maternal devotion of this bird have not been traced back further than the earliest known version of *Physiologus*, which relates that the snake, taking advantage of the mother's absence from the nest in search of food, directed his venom on the wind in the direction of the nest, thereby poisoning the chicks. On her return the mother, distraught at the loss of her brood, flew up into the clouds and struck her side with her wings. The blood which rained down from her side fell upon the young ones lying in the nest and brought them back to life. Bartholomew Anglicus explains what happened after that:

... and then for great bleeding the mother waxeth feeble, and the birds are compelled to pass out of the nest to get themselves meat. And some of them for kind love feed the mother that is feeble, and some are unkind and care not for the mother, and the mother taketh good heed thereto, and when she cometh to her strength, she nourisheth and loveth those birds that fed her in her need, and putteth away her other birds, as unworthy and unkind, and suffereth them not to dwell nor live with her.

Between 1592 and 1599 an Englishman named Sylvester translated into English in decasyllabic verse the work of a man with the imposing name of Guillaume de Saluste, Seigneur Du Bartas. The title of the book and its sequel were *La Semaine*, which recounts the history of the creation of the world, and *La Seconde Semaine*, about the infancy of the world. The story of the pelican, given in this work, runs as follows:

The other, kindly for her tender brood
Tears her own bowels, trilleth out her blood
To heal her young, and in a woundrous sort
Unto her children doth her life transport;

For, finding them by some fell serpent slain,
She rents her breasts and doth upon them rain
Her vital humour; whence recovering heat
They by her death another life do get.

Bartholomew Anglicus also comments on the feeding habits of the pelican, which he regards as somewhat similar to those of humans: 'All that the pelican eateth, he plungeth in water with his foot, and when he hath so plunged it in water, he putteth it into his mouth with his own foot, as it were with an hand. Only the pelican and the popinjay among fowls use the foot instead of an hand.'

While the pelican provides the bestiary writers with an example of parental devotion, another bird, the hoopoe, offers an instance of filial love and care. For when this bird perceives that old age is overtaking its mother and father, it warms them and preens their feathers for them, and licks their eyes as if to repay them for their loving kindness in the days of its own infancy.

In sharp contrast to the maternal or filial affection of these creatures were the unmaternal and unfilial goings-on of the scorpion, whose sting was almost invariably fatal to women and children, but to men only in the morning when the insect first emerged from its hole. Pliny tells us that this creature produced broods of eleven at a time, and that the mother killed all but one of her offspring. This one, more resourceful than the rest, escaped death by perching on her haunches, where it was out of reach of both her bite and her venomous tail. Eventually this lone survivor avenged the death of its brothers and sisters by a downward blow which killed the mother.

The anonymous early thirteenth-century *Ancrene Riwle*, or 'Guide for Anchoresses', compares lechery to the scorpion, offering the following explanation:

The scorpion is a kind of serpent with a face, so it is said, rather like a woman's, while its hind parts are those of a serpent. It makes a show of fairness, practises deception with its head, and stings with its tail. This is lechery. This is the devil's beast which he takes to market and to every other meeting-place and offers for sale, deceiving many, because they see nothing but the fair face or the handsome head. That head is the beginning of the sin of lechery and the pleasure which, while it lasts, seems so sweet. The tail, that is, its end, is sore repentance, and it stings here on earth with the venom of sharp compunction and of penance, and she who finds the tail thus may call herself happy, for the poison will pass away. But if it does not inflict pain here on earth, then the tail with its venomous end is the eternal torment of hell. And is not he a foolish dealer who when he wants to buy a horse or an ox will look only at the head? So, when the devil offers this beast and tries to sell it and asks your soul in return, he always hides the tail while he shows off the head. But walk all round it, and show up the hind parts, and how there is a sting in the tail, and then flee from it at once, before you receive the poison.*

Though the whole animal kingdom was regarded in the early days of the Christian Church as an object-lesson provided by God for mankind, the lesson in some instances was simply an indication of the wonders which the Creator could perform at will, and of his loving kindness in decorating the world so beautifully for the benefit of man.

Some of the creatures noted in the bestiaries were therefore a reflection of man's admiration of the natural world, particularly in regard to some of the birds which were illustrated there. We can imagine the sense of wonder conveyed by the story of the ercinee, a bird native to the forests of Bohemia, whose phosphorescent feathers glowed in the dark, and whose path could be traced in the sky at night as it moved from tree to tree like a ball of light.

No less marvellous was the cinomologus, a bird of Arabia which built its nest on the topmost branches of tall trees and constructed it out of cinnamon. The hunt for this bird's nest was akin to the search for buried treasure, for if a person succeeded in finding and capturing one, he could sell it for a small fortune on account of the spices which it contained. Though the branches on which they perched were so slender that they would not bear the weight of a man, these nests could sometimes be dislodged and brought to the ground by carefully aimed stones.

* Translated into modern English by M. B. Salu, 1955.

A bird admired for its milk-white feathers was the legendary caladrius. This was often to be found in royal households, not only because of its beauty but also because of its special talent for diagnosing whether a sick man would recover or die. It would perch on the bed of the sufferer and turn its back on him if his sickness was going to prove fatal, or face him if he were about to recover. In such instances it would absorb the man's disease, fly with it towards the sun, vomit it in the upper atmosphere and allow it to disperse. This would restore the patient to health.

Equally at home in royal palaces was the peacock, famous for the surpassing beauty of its plumage. Yet its feet were said to be so ugly that they caused it continual embarrassment, and it would shriek loudly every time it caught a glimpse of them.

A bird considered to be regal in its own right was the eagle. Its eyesight was so remarkable that it was believed to see a fish in the depths of the ocean from a vantage point high up in the sky, and also to be able to stare unblinking at the sun. As a test of its wife's fidelity it would take its offspring up to the sun and test its eyesight by making it peer fixedly at it. If the chick's eyes watered, the father would reject it as a bastard. When it reached old age it was said that the eagle's eyes grew dim. In order to counteract the effects of this it would fly so near the sun that it would be scorched by the power of its rays. After that it would seek out a pure fountain, and diving down from the sky, would dip itself three times in the clear water. By this action the youth of the eagle would be restored.

In sharp contrast to the beautiful birds which delighted mankind were various strange snakes which terrified our ancestors. There was, for instance, the cerastes, with horns on its forehead like a ram, which buried itself in the sand with nothing but the horns visible in order to provide a bait for small birds, etc. Stags, they said, were able to suck out these snakes from their holes with a snort and to cure their own ailments by eating them. Other horrifying serpents were various kinds of asp, including the spectaficus, which rots a man away completely with a bite, and the dipsas, or water bucket, whose bite makes a man die of thirst, and whose name, as T. H. White points out, is associated with the modern word dipsomaniac.

Yet another variety is the prester, whose mouth, from which steam gushes, hangs perpetually open. The sting of this snake causes a man to swell to such enormous proportions that he turns putrid and dies.

Snake charmers were able to raise an asp from its hole by muttering charms and playing music on a pipe. Being unwilling to obey this hypnotic summons, the asp was said to press one ear to the ground, stopping the other ear by inserting its own tail into the orifice. In this way it was able to resist the incantation.

The Bestiary of Philip de Thaun adds a further piece of information about the asp:

. . . sometimes they will take the blood of those whom they shall sting;—as was the case with Cleopatra, who was wise in the arts,—she was called queen of the country of Egypt; —she did this wonder, she put them to her teats,—and they milked her so hard that they sucked out the blood;—the queen died of it. . . .

Though snakes were in general hated and feared by men, the adder was specially noted for its love and loyalty to its mate. Bartholomew Anglicus describes its faithfulness:

This slaying adder and venomous hath wit to love and affection, and loveth his mate as it were by love of wedlock, and liveth not well out of her company. Therefore if the one is slain, the other pursueth him that slew the other with so busy wreak and vengeance, that passeth weening. And knoweth the slayer, and reseth on him, be he in never so great company of men and of people, and busieth to slay him, and passeth all difficulties and spaces of ways, and with wreak of the said death of his mate. And is not let, ne put off, but it be by swift flight; or by waters or rivers.

Being fond of moist heat, adders were believed to lie in wait for sleeping men, and if they lay with their mouths open, would seize the opportunity to creep inside. But these activities were sometimes frustrated by a little animal called the saura, of which Bartholomew Anglicus writes:

But against such adders a little beast fighteth that hight Saura, as it were a little ewt, and some men mean that it is a lizard; for when this beast is aware that this serpent is present, he leapeth upon his face that sleepeth, and scratcheth with his feet to wake him, and to warn him of the serpent. And when this little beast waxeth old, his eyen wax blind, and then he goeth into a hole of a wall against the east, and openeth his eyen afterward when the sun is risen, and then his eyen heat and take light.

Snakes in old age could rejuvenate themselves by fasting until their skin became loose, and then sloughing it off by crawling through a tight crevice in the rocks. When thirsty they vomited their venom in a hole from which they could recover it and suck it up again after slaking their thirst at the river. Although they would strike without hesitation at a man who had his clothes on, they were maidishly terrified if they saw a nude one. If the spittle of a fasting man fell upon the snake it would instantly die.

The boa constrictor was, of course, particularly feared because of its size and strength. Solinus, in his *Polyhistor*, explains why it was so strong. The first English translation of this work was published in 1587, and the title page tells us that the translator was 'Arthur Golding, Gent'. His rendering of the information about the boa constrictor reads as follows:

First it seeketh after Heardes of mylde kyne, and what Cowe soever yeeldeth most milke, her dugs dooth he draw. And battling with continuall sucking of her, in processe of tyme hee so stuffeth out hymselfe with overglutting hym tyll hee bee readie to burste, that at the last no power is able to withstande hys hugenesse.

Pythons were the traditional enemy of the elephant, and would hide themselves in the branches of trees along paths which the elephant was known to frequent. From this vantage point they could drop down on the luckless elephant and shackle its legs in their coils, in order to prevent it from rubbing them with great force against rocks and the bark of trees. When the elephant retaliated with its trunk, the python would poke its head into the elephant's nostrils, preventing it from breathing and wounding it in the tenderest part. They often attacked its eyes, and elephants as a result were frequently found blind, exhausted and starving.

Pliny also tells us how pythons sought the cold blood of elephants in particularly hot weather:

> . . . they submerge themselves in rivers and lie in wait for the elephants when drinking, and rising up coil round the trunk and imprint a bite inside the ear, because that place only cannot be protected by the trunk; and that the snakes are so large that they can hold the whole of an elephant's blood, and so they drink the elephants dry, and these when drained collapse in a heap and the serpents being intoxicated are crushed by them and die with them.

Solinus goes even further, claiming that 'they never sette upon them, but when they have drunk theyr bellies full, to the intent when their vaynes be well stuffed with moysture, they may suck the more out of them. . . .'

Just why our ancestors found it necessary to codify their errors in this way is an interesting subject for speculation. Already we have probed some of the reasons and have seen how man's overwhelming desire for knowledge, not only in regard to those matters relating to his own environment but also respecting far-away places which he had never seen for himself, urged him to seek new information and to chart both the known and the unknown, using invention where reason and intelligent observation failed. We have noted the way in which man's deep-seated need of a compelling religion, both to tide him over present difficulty in a precarious world and to offer him hope of a hereafter, was accompanied in the new age of Christianity by the remnants of pagan habit with its insistence on some kind of magical formula as a defence against the forces of evil in the world, and how this proved a powerful incentive in the composition of the bestiaries. We have seen too how the Greek ideals of reasoned judgment based on careful observation, as advocated and put into practice by Aristotle, were rejected by the early Christian fathers in their search for moral and Christian values in a precarious existence,

13. The unicorn at the fountain; detail of the Flemish tapestry, 'The Hunt of the Unicorn', *c.* 1500.

14. The unicorn and the maiden; detail of a French tapestry, late fifteenth century.

15. The unicorn and the naked virgin. Early thirteenth-century manuscript.

16. The beaver castrates itself before the hunter. From Harley Manuscript 4751.

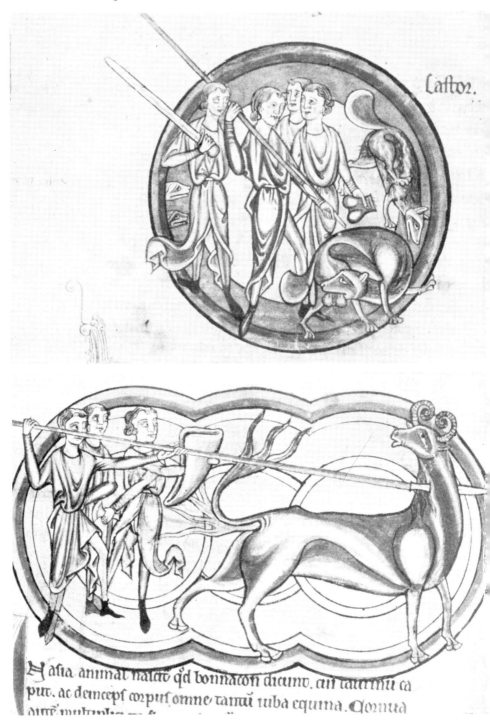

Castor.

Nasia animal natat qd bonnacon dicunt. aut taurinu caput. ac deinceps corpus omne/tainu tuba equina. Cornua

17. The bonnacon emits a fart. From Harley Manuscript 4751.

Est animal qd dr elephans· in q̃ n̄· est concupiscencia coit· Elephantem
grei a magnitudine corporis nocatur quod formam mon-
tis pferat· Grece enim mons· elipho dr· Apd indos aut a uoce barro uo-
cat̄· Unde·e·ox ugr a barrit· et dentes eī ebur· Rostrū aut ptosada ul' pmusada
dr· qm̃ illo pabula ori admouet· et·e· angui similis uallo munit eburneo· Hul-
lū eial gñdi uidet̄· In eis eū ipse et india lignea trib; collocati camiq; de muro
ualdis dimicant· Intellectu et memoria uita uigrǵt· gregatim incedūt· murē
fugiūt· auersi coeunt· Biennio au̇ pariuriūt· n̄ amplius q̃m semel gigniūt·
n̄ plures si n̄ unū· Uiuiūt au̇ annos trecentos· Si aūte uolurit facere fili-
os·uadīt ad oriente· ipe ptadisū· et·e· ibi arbor que nocat̄ mandragora· et ua-
dit cū femina sua que pu̇ accipit de arbore et dat masclo suo· et seducit eum
toū manducat· Statimq; in utro capit· Cū au̇ pariendi tempus uenit in stang-
nū· et aqua uenit usq; ad ubera matris· Elephans aut custodit eam parturien-
te· qa draco·e· inimic̃ elephanti· si aū inuenit serpente occidit eī· que gricat̄
toū morbū· Est eū formidabilis canus elephans· cui nunc nimer· h̄ e· naca
eī si ceciderit n̄ potest surge· Qaddit aū cū se inclinat in arbore ut dormiat· n̄
cū h̄e iuncturas genidos· Uenator aū incidit arbore mediaci· in elephans cū se
inclinauit· simul cū arbore cadat· Cadens aū clamat fonti· et statim magnu
elephans urit et n̄ potest cū leuare· Tunc clamant ambo et ueniūt· xij· elephā-
tes et n̄ possunt cū leuare q̃ ceciderit· Deinde clamāt oms· et stati ueuit pusillus
elephans et mittit os sui ad pmusada subt magnū elephante· et eleuat cū.

19. Satyr. From *The Historie of Foure-footed Beastes*.

qin ita manluecii.uc non lint magni tadioi.jnc uinial dadcic
jlpinger.uillofe inarmif acdocilef ad fernif obluriore.

Sunt ꝯquof uocan
trof facie admodum
grata gelticulatif motibz in
quiete. Callitricef toto pene
afpectu acterif differunt.
Jn facie barba elt. Lata cau
da. hof capere non elt ardu
um fed proferre rarum.

Hecque uiuunt inaltero quam in ethiopico hoc ꞓ fuo celo

20. Satyr. From Cambridge University Library Manuscript 11.4.26.

22. The whale mistaken for an island. From Harley Manuscript 3244.

ft belua in mari que grece aſpido delone dicaẽ Aſpido
Laune ũ aſpido teſtudo. Otere etam dicta. ob ſece.
minrannant corpozif. eſt eñi ſicut ille q̃ ercepti

23. The hyena was thought to break open coffins and devour the dead. From *The Royal Bestiary*.

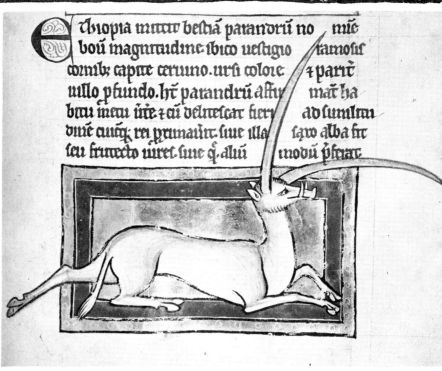

Chiopia mictir bestiā parandrū no   miē
boū magnitudine. sbico uestigio   /tamosic
cornib; capite ceruino. ursi coloie   /paric̄
uillo pfundo. hr̄ parandrū astu   mat ha
bitu metu iūre. ꞇ cū delitescat fieri   ad similitu
diuē cuiꝗ rei pximailit. siue illa   sꞇʒo alba sit
seu srucecto uiret. siue ꝗ̄ aluī   modū pferat

24. The yale, a creature able to swivel its horns independently. From
The Royal Bestiary.

where the coming of the Kingdom of God was expected almost daily.

There was a further factor which we have not yet taken into account. This was mankind's delight in bestowing on dumb animals the characteristics of human beings, usually with some kind of didactic purpose in mind. Such characteristics were exhibited in animal fables, the most famous exponent of which was Aesop, who composed his tales in about the year 600 B.C. We do not know whether he ever wrote down his stories, but versions of them were later recorded both in Greek and in Latin, before being translated into many other languages.

The fable was popular in the Middle Ages, and in addition to those of Aesop examples by many other authors were widely circulated during that period. The well-known tale of Reynard the Fox was written down in about the tenth century A.D., and gained wide currency in many tongues. In this story Reynard successfully outwits a number of other animals including the wolf, the bear and the lion. Chaucer too provided us with a very famous example of the beast fable in 'The Nun's Priest's Tale' where Chanticleer, the cock who rules a roost of seven hens, dreams that a fearful beast is murdering him. His favourite wife, putting it down to 'vapours in the belly', volunteers to cure him with an emetic:

> Worms for a day or two I'll have to give
> As a digestive, then your laxative.
> Centaury, fumitory, caper-spurge
> And hellebore will make a splendid purge. . . .

Chanticleer, indignant that his dream is not taken as a serious portent, and offended by her offer of a laxative, which he regards as poisonous, recounts the story of a man who dreams that his friend is murdered and hidden in a dung-heap, later discovering that the dream had come true. Despite his premonition, Chanticleer's vanity betrays him into the hands of Sir Russell Fox, and it is only by a piece of equal cunning that Chanticleer manages to escape.

What distinguishes the fable from other literary forms is

that it relates incidents in the lives of animals who speak
and act like human beings. Unlike the animals in these
fables, who are usually personalized by a name, the characteristic actions of animals described in the bestiaries are not
individual but common to all animals of that species. One
essential difference between the fable and the bestiary is that
the former, though presented as fact, was not expected to be
believed but merely to prove both entertaining and instructive, whereas the bestiary accounts were offered as simple
truth by a writer who knew that his moral and zoological
authority would not be challenged.

Largely as a result of the widespread popularity of
allegory and fable, certain animals came to be recognized for
various human characteristics. The ass, for instance, was
noted for stupidity, the bee and the ant for industry and
efficient colonization, the lion for majesty and the dove for
gentleness.

The fox was noted for its cunning not only in the fables
but also in the bestiaries. *Physiologus* relates that when this
beast has been unsuccessful in his hunting expeditions and
feels the pangs of hunger coming on, he rolls himself in red
mud so that he appears to be stained with his own blood,
and then lies on his back on the ground, holding his breath
for as along as possible, so that he appears to be dead. While
he lies there without sign of life and with his tongue hanging
out, the fowls of the air fly down and sit upon his stomach,
thinking that he has been killed. When their usual guard
has been relaxed in this way, the fox suddenly springs to
life, seizes them and gobbles them up. The fox is likened to
the devil, who lures mankind and overpowers him in an
unguarded moment.

There were, of course, abundant precedents in the Bible
for using examples from the animal kingdom to point a
moral lesson. Most people, for instance, will recognize the
following piece of advice offered in the Book of Proverbs: *
'Go to the ant, thou sluggard: consider her ways and be
wise.'

And, predictably, the bestiarists took up this challenge,

* Prov. vi. 6.

featuring this little creature, so well known to us all, in their work. Or is it, after all, as well known to us as we have always believed? For the truth about this tiny, insignificant creature is quite remarkable. Most of us are familiar with the organization of the ant colony around the winged queen. We may even be aware that the queen selects a single mate with whom she embarks on a kind of honeymoon flight. What is not so well known is that during this flight she receives a supply of male sperm which can last for as much as fifteen years. It is scarcely surprising that after this exhausting operation the male, having outlived his usefulness, simply dies. Nor will the average reader be aware that the males of the species are produced from unfertilized eggs.

Such advanced data were not, of course, available to the bestiary writers, but it is interesting to find that though over 5,000 species of ants have been identified, our medieval ancestors give an account of a variety of ants undreamed of by modern zoologists. For the Ethiopian ant, according to Solinus, is as large as a mastiff and incredibly fierce. This beast collects gold from the bed of a river, driving men away and guarding its hoard closely. However much they covet it, men are unable to take it away from the Ethiopian ant unless they employ the following strategy.

First, they starve a mare which has recently foaled, and on the third day they bind a little basket to her back. Then they lead her past the river containing the gold and leave her to graze in a pasture nearby. While she is satisfying three days' hunger by cropping the grass greedily, the ants discover the basket, and finding it ideal as a cell, proceed to load it with gold. But when the mare has satisfied her hunger she hears her colt calling to her and gallops back to it, taking the gold with her. On her return the owner is able to take off the basket and keep the whole of the gold for himself.

Another variety of ant was the formicaleon, concerning which Philip de Thaun writes: 'It is a very little beast, which lays itself in the dust, where the ant approaches and does it great outrage. But of this matter I will say no more.' The precise nature of the outrage which occasions such an abrupt change of subject is left to our imaginations.

These two examples from the bestiaries illustrate two quite separate kinds of misconception. In the case of the formicaleon, error easily arises because the creature is too tiny for minute observation with the naked eye. The Ethiopian ant, on the other hand, illustrates the imaginative tale told of creatures in a land far away. In stories of this kind the fancy could range at will, and Ethiopia was traditionally a country where all sorts of monstrosities flourished.

Robert Browning, in his poem *The Pied Piper of Hamelin*, portrays children following the piper to a land where the animals were familiar, but decorated:

> The sparrows were brighter than peacocks here,
> And their dogs outran the fallow deer,
> And honey bees had lost their stings,
> And horses were born with eagle's wings.

The story of the Ethiopian ant is in the same sort of tradition, the creature being thousands of times larger than life, and associated with virtually unattainable treasure in the bargain.

The treatment of the goat was rather different, for here men were dealing with a common domestic animal which would have been an everyday sight in all the countries where *Physiologus* and the bestiaries flourished. The appearance of the goat was not decorated in any way, yet nevertheless it had various interesting characteristics. It had a strong preference for mountain-tops, moving higher and higher as it ruminated, and selecting with its keen eyes none but the tastiest shoots. If wounded it hurried to the herb dittany, knowing that if it tasted its leaves it would be cured. From its vantage point in the highest mountain crags it could spy out the approach of man from a safe distance, and with its sharp eyes could discriminate between an ordinary traveller and a hunter. The bestiary writers likened it to God the Holy Goat who looked down from on high and detected the nature of approaching man.

It is rather curious to find the goat associated with God in this way, for other stories link this animal with lust and, by the same analogy, with the devil. Like most horned beasts it had a reputation for lechery, and it is interesting to note that the horns of the cuckolded husband had been taken over at some stage in the Middle Ages from the brow of the lascivious adulterer.

There was no direct association between the goat and treasure of any kind, but there was an indirect link. For even more potent than the urine of the lynx with its capacity for solidifying into a precious stone was the blood of the goat, which was so powerful that it was said to be able to dissolve the hardest of all minerals, the adamant.

Readers may have been puzzled by pictures produced in the Middle Ages in which Capricorn, the goat, is portrayed as a goat in front only, having the tail of a serpent, usually coiled, behind. Sometimes the front and rear ends of this strange composite beast are joined with a knot in the middle. The serpentine tail is said to represent the torment which Christ will inflict upon sinners, and the knot signifies the sin by which men are bound.

The salamander was, of course, less familiar than the goat, yet it is another of the many examples of real animals concerning which popular misconceptions grew up. This creature really is poisonous, but is in no way dangerous to man. Nevertheless it was believed to be so venomous that if it wound itself around the trunk of a tree it would poison all the fruit, and kill anyone who ate it. It was believed to be so cold that it could not only pass through fire unharmed but also put out the flames. The skin of this creature was said to be covered with fine hair from which asbestos could be made. T. H. White points out that an Emperor of India had a suit made from a thousand salamander skins, and gives the following quotation from Caxton's *Myrrour of the World*, 1481: 'This Salemandre berith wulle, of which is made cloth and gyrdles that may not brenne in the fyre.'

Lack of opportunity for observation was an almost overwhelming obstacle in the case of the whale, and this was doubtless one reason why men had to fall back on their imaginations in respect of this beast. One medieval miniature brings out this difficulty very well, for it depicts a limner waiting patiently with his parchment and quill by the seashore, where he is rewarded with the glimpse of the whale's head needed to complete his picture (Plate 4).

The whale was accordingly thought to have some very curious habits. It was its custom to float with its back just above the surface of the water so that vegetation grew on it, and because it looked so much like an island, sailors would anchor their ships beside it and disembark onto its back. Here they would light a fire, and when the heat penetrated to the beast, it would plunge instantly to the sea-bed, drowning all those who had climbed upon it (Plate 22).

The whale was claimed to exude such a sweet odour that it would lure small fish into its mouth and swallow them. Guillaume le Clerc, who wrote his *Bestiare Divin* in Norman French in the early thirteenth century, points out that in this he resembles the devil, for:

> He sets a bait for them,
> Which at first smells very sweet,
> As is some carnal pleasure like
> Having a fair woman in bed . . .
> Which at first smells very sweet,
> But then ends in bitterness.

Apparently the female whale was not allowed to conceive from copulation with another whale, but solaced herself instead with the little pilot fish.

Ideas about the appearance of the crocodile seem to have been equally strange, and for much the same reason. The bestiary of Guillaume le Clerc describes it as follows:

> The crocodile is a wild beast
> And dwells ever on the bank
> Of that river which is named Nile.
> It is like an ox in some respects.
> It is full twenty cubitts long,
> And is as stout as the trunk of a tree.
> Four feet it has and great claws
> And teeth sharp and cutting.

The expression 'crocodile tears' is still in current use. It originates from the belief that crocodiles slew men and wept while eating them. Some reports tell us that the tears showed repentance, but Asterious, the Bishop of Amasia, writing in about the year A.D. 400, offers a different explanation: 'These, they say, lament over the heads of men they have eaten, and weep over the relics of the slaughter, not feeling penitent for what has happened, but (as it seems to me) bewailing the lack of flesh on the head as unsuitable for eating.'

On the other hand crocodiles themselves came in for rough treatment at the hands of those races bold enough to hunt them. Aelian explains that the people of the City of Apollo used to catch them in a net, hang them on trees and flog them until they whimpered and wept. According to Herodotus, one method of catching the crocodile was to lure it with a live pig, and as soon as it reached land, to plaster its eyes with mud, after which it was an easy matter to kill it. Herodotus also tells us that in Thebes the crocodile was venerated, and it was the custom to keep one and tame it: 'They adorn his ears with earrings of molten stone or gold, and put bracelets on his forepaws, giving him a set portion of bread, with a certain number of victims; and after having treated him with greatest possible attention while alive, they embalm him when he dies and bury him in a sacred repository.'

Pliny relates that when the crocodile is sated with food, it opens its mouth to allow a little bird, the trochilus, to hop inside and pick its teeth, consuming the morsels of food which it finds there. This gives the crocodile a very pleasurable sensation. (Small birds may be seen today engaging in this mutually beneficial operation.) Pliny continues: '... and the ichneumon watches for it to be overcome by sleep in the middle of this gratification and darts like a javelin through the throat so opened and gnaws out the belly.'

Another dangerous enemy of the crocodile was the hydrus, which Topsell (1608) pictures as a many-headed serpent (Plate 9). This mythical water serpent was said to slide into the mouth of the sleeping crocodile, and, having devoured its entrails, to gnaw its way out through the belly. The asp penetrated the crocodile in much the same way, but first coated itself liberally with mud. Some claimed that this was in order that it could slide more easily down the gullet of its enemy, and others that it allowed the mud to harden so that it would be as hard and sharp as a sword.

However low mere beasts might sink in their behaviour, man could, of course, be even beastlier. Sir John Mandeville explains the extraordinary religious custom practised in Ethiopia, where the ox was worshipped as a god. The king took a sacred ox with him wherever he went, reserving its dung in one vessel of gold and its urine in another. And every day he offered it to the archbishop to be blessed.

And than the kyng put his hand into the donge and takith thereof, and robith his theth, his brest, his forhed and his visage; thanne with gret reverence takyth (more) of the mok, and robbyth hym so that he shulde ben fulfyld of that holy oxe, and that he shal ben blyssid thour vertu of that holy thing. And aftyr the kyng othere lordis and pryncis shuln don on the same maner, and aftyr hem seruantys and othere menere men as longe as ony thing lastyth thereof.

In the next chapter we pass to a field in which men can behave in an even beastlier fashion, namely with regard to animal medicines and aphrodisiacs.

CHAPTER SEVEN

Animal Medicines, Charms and Aphrodisiacs

'FFRIE EARTHWORMES wth goosegreasse then strayne the same and drop a lytell therof into the deafe and payned eares warminge the same and so vsse yt hallfe a dossen times at the least a trewe medison probatm.' This remedy for deafness appears in the diaries of an Elizabethan Englishman called Philip Henslowe. An alternative cure is also noted: 'Take antes eages and stampe them and strayne them through a cloth then take swines greasse ore cnotte grasse stampe the same and take the Jusse and myxe wth other straininge of the eges and put in to the eare searten dropes yt will healpe and owld deafnes yf god permet pbatm.'

It might be imagined that the man who kept a record of such unlikely remedies in his diaries could have been nothing more than a credulous country bumpkin. Yet in fact Philip Henslowe was one of the shrewdest businessmen in Elizabethan London. A dyer by trade, he owned not only the Boar's Head Inn in Southwark, and various profitable lodging houses of doubtful reputation, but also 'stews' in the Cock Lane area, a notable resort for prostitutes. Stews were bath-houses which had existed from medieval times, and flourished as an alternative to brothels, for here the oldest profession could be practised under the thin guise of legitimate business.

Henslowe was one of the first to realize that there were great opportunities for profit in the public theatre, and in 1584 he purchased the land near Southwark Bridge where the little Rose playhouse stood. Over the years he had interests in various playhouses, including the Rose, the Swan and the Fortune Theatre in Golden Lane, Cripplegate Without. Besides owning a substantial share in the Paris Garden, which was used for bear-baiting, he obtained the office of Master of the Royal Game of Bears, Bulls and Mastiffs, looking after the royal lions and bears as a sideline. One of his methods of accumulating wealth was to lend money to actors, to be repaid with interest from their wages; another was to buy direct from dramatists plays which were not only put on in his own theatres but also hired out to other companies.

This was the kind of man who put his faith in fried earthworms and strained ants' eggs. The notebooks are really business records of Henslowe's theatrical activities, but paper was a precious commodity in Elizabethan times, and various miscellaneous entries, too valuable to be lost, got in among the notes of plays and players. The remedies for ear trouble are not in Henslowe's own hand but were presumably copied out by a member of his household.

Henslowe was not just giving way to an amiable weakness for eccentric antidotes. In common with his contemporaries as well as his forbears, he really believed in the efficacy of his cures and preventives, and there is no doubt at all that the remedies were recorded not just from idle curiosity but because he intended to use them if the occasion ever arose. Many of the cures used in Henslowe's day, both animal and herbal, dated from the pre-Christian era. Whether they were gleaned from ancient medical authorities, written down in family recipe books or simply passed on by word of mouth from one generation to the next, centuries of use had made them seem reliable.

If after trial the remedies were seen not to work there were always other factors to blame: the influence of the stars, the malevolence of witches, the will of God. But the fact that every complaint prompted half a dozen palliatives suggest that there were limits to people's readiness to put their trust in any one of them.

Fifteen hundred years before Henslowe, Pliny had had

other recipes for ear trouble, equally bizarre: 'the seminal fluid of a hog caught as it drips from a sow before it can touch the ground', for example. Alternatively he suggests treating the diseased ear with a concoction of centipedes boiled in leek-juice, or with the juice crushed from the head of a black-beetle. This last had to be soaked up in a piece of wool and the wool plugged into the ear, but Pliny is careful to warn against leaving it there too long as otherwise maggots might breed in it.

Pliny also reports that crickets were thought to be very efficacious for treating earache. He was personally sceptical about this since the sole basis for the belief was that they walked backwards, bored into the ground and chirruped at night. The procedure for catching a cricket was rather complicated: 'They hunt it with an ant tied to a hair and put into the cricket's hole, first blowing the dust away lest it bury itself, and so when the ant has embraced it the cricket is pulled out.'

Even from the few examples so far quoted it is clear that there was no real advance from the methods of the first century to those of the sixteenth. For the fact is that the graph registering advance in medical knowledge does not curve smoothly up from prehistory to the modern age. In the period covered by this book—from classical antiquity to the seventeenth century—progress was painfully slow, and there were regressions. The discoveries which have revolutionized medicine and more than doubled life expectancy were all still to come, so that from Hesiod in the eighth century B.C. to Sir Thomas Browne nearly two and a half thousand years later the general picture of disease and cure is very much the same.

There was heavy dependence on preparations of an animal nature for curative or cosmetic purposes, and no major treatise on the animal kingdom could have been complete without its quota of charms and remedies. To the Christian of the Middle Ages God had made animals for the benefit of mankind, and one of these benefits was their use in charms and cures. Bartholomew Anglicus points this out: 'Also bestys ben ordenyed not oonly for meete of the body: but also for remedye of euylles/and also for many maner of medycynes . . .' *

But animal remedies were not exclusive to practising Christians. They had been in use in pagan societies as far back in time as we can trace, and were often based on the age-old principle of the nastier the better. Examples of revolting substances used in ancient Rome for various ailments include vulture brains with oil and cedar resin, rubbed over the head and into the nostrils to cure headache, gravy from roasted raven's lung to anoint itching eruptions of the private parts, and tree-maggots to plug hollow teeth.

In the first century A.D. a popular writer like Pliny was catering for men who were prepared to believe that if they plucked the tongues from live frogs and placed them over the beating hearts of their wives while they slept they would act as a kind of truth drug. Hardly less strange and revolting was a tenth-century remedy for eye diseases: 'For swollen eyes, take a live crab, put his eyes out and put him back in the water alive. Hang the eyes round the neck of the patient: he will soon be well.'

Remedies of this kind were thought to be effective only as long as the mutilated animal remained alive. Apart from their gruesomeness, these examples illustrate two features which cropped up again and again in prescriptions: the reliance on charms; and the 'sympathetic magic' which presumed that if some part of the body was not functioning satisfactorily, a ritual involving the corresponding part of a healthy animal could correct it. Mankind was a long way from today's transplant surgery, which goes to the lengths of inserting parts of animals into ailing human beings, but the assumption, explicit today, that man and animal have much in common seems implicitly to have been recognized by our ancestors.

A straightforward association of ideas of this kind was probably the logic behind ancient Roman attempts to cure palpitations by eating boiled hyena heart and to mend broken bones by swallowing ash from the jawbone of a wild boar. For similar reasons men suffering from stone in the bladder expected to be cured by eating the bladder of a wild boar,

* *De Proprietatibus Res*, 1372, bk 18, ch. 1.

though it is interesting to note that women with the same complaint were recommended to eat the bladder not of the boar but of the sow.

Burnt sow's bladder taken in drink or the testicle of a hare were both recommended for sufferers from incontinence of urine. Occasionally, however, the association of ideas depended on the outside agency which caused the ailment, so that although the foam of a horse was generally believed to have soothing properties it was particularly recommended for soreness in the groin caused by excessive riding.

The system by which men decided which animals were to be exploited in the cause of medicine is not easy to grasp, but there are hints here and there that it was not entirely haphazard or whimsical, and that beliefs about animals described in earlier chapters lay at the back of it.

For instance, a favourite remedy for a whole range of eye afflictions was the dung of a she-goat, coated with wax, to be swallowed by the sufferer at the new moon. The reason why the dung of this animal was so highly regarded for ophthalmia was that the herbs which formed a part of its normal diet were believed to keep it permanently free from eye disease and, as we have already seen in chapter six, the goat was thought by the bestiarists to have exceptionally keen vision. Some people swore by goat's dung with honey not only as a cure but also as a preventive of eye diseases, though others claimed that hare's dung in raisin wine or a fox tongue worn as an amulet was equally beneficial. While the goat-dung remedy had some attempt at cause-and-effect reasoning behind it, the alternatives appear to rely entirely on simple trust.

Another sort of sympathetic magic—depending on unlikeness rather than likeness—comes from ancient Rome. Designed to cure enuresis, it was a complicated piece of ritual, involving divine assistance, a medicament, and what seems a version of psychiatric therapy. After swallowing down a draught of the ashes of a boar's genitals in sweet wine, the patient was ordered to urinate in a dog's bed, at the same time offering a prayer to the gods that he might not make water, as a dog does, in his own bed.

It is less easy to see why a man with a headache expected it to go away if he tied the genitals of a fox round his forehead, or why sufferers from colic hoped for relief if they tied a lark's heart to the thigh. Topsell (1607) went in for stronger measures. His favourite remedy for this ailment was the dung of a horse fed with oats and barley (but on no account with grass) in half a pint of wine, to be drunk down, preferably all at one go.

Patients who spat blood could be greatly benefited by drinking the blood of an ox or cow, though this could be taken only in moderation, for ox-blood was thought to be highly toxic, and Themistocles was said to have committed suicide by drinking it in the year 449 B.C. W. T. Fernie, in *Animal Simples*, notes that prussic acid is obtainable from blood, and it has been suggested that this may once have been termed ox-blood. He points out that, curiously enough, draughts of blood were once very popular, and quotes the following, from an unspecified source:

Bullocks' blood is now [1872] in vogue among the Parisians for anaemia, and pulmonary consumption. It is a curious sight to view the number of patients of both sexes and all ranks and ages who flock to the slaughter-house every morning. Young ladies take the blood eagerly, and I have heard them say they prefer it to cod-liver-oil.

Disagreeable though cod-liver oil may be, it cannot compare for sheer nastiness with most ancient animal potions. Perhaps the most striking feature of these preparations was the often highly insanitary and almost always obnoxious nature of their components. The rich could have their remedies gilded to disguise the disagreeable animal substances inside, but for the poor there was often no better way of hiding these nauseating concoctions from their eyes than drinking down their medicine through straws under cover of darkness.

Even Pliny, who recommended without a qualm the use of bits of spider as a female contraceptive, and laying earthworms on women's breasts to draw out pus, could not contemplate some of his own remedies without a shudder. It seems that he drew the line at the use of bugs, though he lists a number of cures in which they feature, adding: 'And yet some actually anoint the eyes with bugs pounded in salt and woman's milk.' Yet what disgusted Pliny even more than all the other obnoxious substances which he describes were black beetles, used in a variety of cures: 'Even to hear these remedies mentioned makes me feel sick; but heaven help us! Diodorus says that he had given these beetles with resin and honey even in cases of jaundice and orthopnoea. So much power has the art of medicine to prescribe any medicament it may wish.'

The nastiness had a purpose, however. Revolting substances, such as the raw organs of animals or urine and excrement, both animal and human, were powerful means of driving out the demons thought to be responsible for much physical illness. Robert Burton, in his *Anatomy of Melancholy*, quotes from Jason Pratensis:

. . . the devil, being a slender incomprehensible spirit, can easily insinuate and wind himself into human bodies, and, cunningly couched in our bowels, vitiate our healths, terrify our souls with fearful dreams, and shake our mind with furies . . . These unclean spirits settled in our bodies, and now mixed with our melancholy humours, do triumph as it were, and sport themselves as in another heaven.

In case this was not authority enough, he also cites Taurelles:

By clancular * poisons he (the devil) can infect the bodies, and hinder the operations of the bowels, though we perceive it not.

Fortunately the answer to such demonic invasion was readily available. The patient had only to ensure that he drank, ate or otherwise absorbed something disgusting enough and the devil would be driven out.

The use of urine in medicine in the Middle Ages was ridiculed by Chaucer in the 'Words of the Host to the Physician' in *The Canterbury Tales*:

* secret.

> God's blessing on you, Doctor, not forgetting
> Your various urinals and chamber pots,
> Bottles, medicaments, and cordial tots
> And boxes brimming all with panaceas,
> God's blessing on them all and St Maria's.

In addition to its diagnostic functions urine was thought to have magic properties and to be an excellent specific for a whole range of ailments. Topsell in his *Historie of Foure-footed Beastes* provides an illustration in which urine is both the subject of the complaint and its cure:

> To provoke urine when a man's yard * is stopt, there is nothing so excellent as the dung or filth which proceedeth from the urine which a Horse hath made, being mingled with wine, and then strained, and afterwards poured into the Nostrils of the party so vexed.

If boiled down to half its original quantity with a leek in new earthenware, urine would drive worms out from the ears of the patient. No doubt this was a particularly popular remedy, for people once had a great horror of worms, snakes, etc., creeping in through the various orifices of the body while a person was sound asleep. 'There are some,' Topsell writes in *The Historie of Foure-footed Beastes*, appealing to antique and therefore reliable authority, 'which will assure us, that if a man be troubled with belly worms, or have a Serpent crept into his belly, if he take but the sweat of a Horse being mingled with his urine, and drink it, it will presently cause the Worms or the Serpents to issue forth.' Mixed with the white of an egg, urine could be applied to sunburn, and if matured for a long period and then mixed with ashes of oyster shell it could be used to anoint rashes and running ulcers on the bodies of infants. Whether infants ever managed to survive the cure would seem questionable to the modern reader.

Urine was also believed to cure ulcers, skin complaints and afflictions of the anus. For leprous sores on the face the urine of an ass could be used at the rising of the Dog Star.

---

* A wonderfully self-confident word meaning *penis* which nobody should be surprised to find used in the age of the padded codpiece.

If ass's water was not readily to hand, any kind of urine would do instead. This remedy was probably used very often, for among mankind's perennial fears was that of contracting one of the various plagues which periodically swept across the known world. Thucydides reports one such outbreak which ravaged towns and villages near Athens in the year 430 B.C. Its precise nature remains obscure, but among its horrifying effects was gangrene of the hands, feet, eyeballs and genitals.

So great was the fear of contagion of this kind that many people were turned into vagrant outcasts, not only by their neighbours but even by their own closest relatives. Ironically this was not always because they had contracted a contagious plague but simply on account of faulty diagnosis. It is likely, for instance, that many people who were classed as lepers were in fact suffering from syphilis, which, though serious in itself, would certainly not have warranted such drastic and ruthless measures as turning them away from the towns and hamlets where they lived. Syphilis was rife in Europe from the fifteenth century onwards, when it suddenly broke out in Naples. Prostitution was widespread at that period, and Rome was only one of a number of cities which collected a large revenue in the taxes levied on brothels. Another source of infection was the public baths, which were often scenes of debauchery, with mixed bathing in the nude and bacchanalian feasting and drinking on the premises. Small wonder that people clutched at any possible remedy for the disfiguring sores which they contracted there, especially when the remedy was as readily available as their own urine.

There was one major problem which had to be overcome in collecting the urine needed for these various cures, for at least until Christianity had finally conquered the old multi-theistic beliefs, it was generally believed that if any of the gods happened to see a person passing water, he would be offended, and in his anger might invalidate the cure. No doubt this was a reason which often sprang to mind when the remedy failed to produce the desired effect. Hesiod accordingly recommended that people should always urinate against some object that would act as a screen, to prevent their nakedness from giving offence to the deities.

Dung was equally nauseating and therefore played almost as important a part as urine in primitive medicine. It could be offered to the patient in a variety of ways: either fresh, or dried and pounded, or reduced to ash. It could be mixed with drink or other substances to disguise the flavour, applied as an ointment or worn as an amulet.

Sufferers from cataract, for example, could smear the eye with wolf dung, stone in the bladder could be relieved by mouse droppings rubbed into the belly, and the man who inadvertently swallowed a bone could dislodge it from his throat by rubbing cat's dung into the affected part. Perhaps this remedy achieved its effect by making the patient vomit —the most probable result of such a practice. Sufferers from flatulence were promised relief if they restricted themselves to a menu of snails; but anyone too weak-willed to adhere to a diet could instead drink white hen's dung boiled in hyssop, or alternatively could take calf's dung mulled in wine. It is interesting to note that oxen who suffered from flatulence were said to obtain relief from a human bone inserted into a hole bored in its horns.

To this day warts bring out in people a sneaking belief in magic, perhaps dating from the time when such protuberances were believed to be 'witches' marks', the teats used by witches to suckle the toads, cats, and so forth which were their familiars, or perhaps merely because warts appear, flourish and disappear in a fashion disconcerting to the lay mind. Many sufferers will have been recommended to rub their warts with a piece of steak which must then be buried, preferably under an oak tree. Or they may have been advised to gather one white pebble for each wart, put them in a black draw-string purse and bury the purse at a crossroads. The warts would then be transferred to anyone unlucky enough to unearth the purse.

Since such beliefs have survived even the onslaught of science and the National Health Service, it is scarcely surprising that our ancestors, unblessed by research, held beliefs no less extraordinary. Wart-sufferers of the first century A.D. would probably have been advised to anoint themselves with a liberal application of the dung of an ass mixed with its urine. However mistaken the belief in the efficacy of such a wart-salve, it was at least a genuine attempt to treat the affected part with something thought to have curative properties, whereas the two 'modern' methods mentioned rely on nothing but magic for their value.

As well as excrement and urine, such bodily fluids as blood and sweat figure large in the repertory of ancient physicians. Specifics for diarrhoea included draughts of stag's blood, the ashes of wild boar's dung in warm wine, or, marginally less distasteful, a dose of ashes of bull's horn in water.

But the products of the body—and particularly the human body—connected with sex and reproduction were held in special awe as powerful curative substances. Male semen was one such example, believed to be highly effective in the treatment of stings, especially those of the scorpion. Woman's milk was another. It could ease a variety of ills, from removing the madness caused by drinking henbane to acting as an astringent to the bowels. Nicander favoured young girl's milk for aconite poisoning, considering it effective for a man when 'The top of the belly is gripped with pain . . . while from his streaming eyes drips the moisture; and his belly sore shaken vainly throws up wind, and much of it settles below about his mid-navel; and in his head is a grievous weight. . . .' *

However unlikely it may sound to us today, woman's milk was also prescribed for nausea. Anybody who was unlucky enough to be squirted in the eyes with the venom of a toad could bathe them in woman's milk as an antidote. If mixed with honey and the urine of a child before puberty in equal proportions, woman's milk would bring worms from the ears of the patient.

Most mysterious of all these products of the sexual system was menstrual fluid. This was considered important in controlling various kinds of infestation. According to Metrodorus, the second-century B.C. philosopher and statesman

* *Alexipharmaca*, Ll. 16, in *The Poems and Poetical Fragments*.

quoted by Pliny, the women of Cappadocia once cured a
plague of Spanish fly by walking through the fields with
their skirts raised above their buttocks. Menstruating
women who walked naked about the countryside could
apparently exterminate caterpillars, beetles and other pests;
and no doubt many a farmer was only too glad to employ
women to carry out this task under his personal supervision.

One of the most fashionable afflictions during the Middle
Ages—or at any rate one of the most emphasized in
medieval medical textbooks—was epilepsy. A certain respect
was due to this disease because many well-known people,
including Julius Caesar, had suffered from it.

According to St Augustine, epilepsy was one of a group
of illnesses which would afflict children conceived on
certain forbidden occasions. The moral, presumably, was
that men and women should abstain from sex on Saturdays,
or on the eve of certain other religious festivals, as any
children begotten on such occasions would inevitably be
born with major defects. But for those whose parents had
ignored the warnings and who were consequently born
epileptic, St Augustine recommended the testicles of a
bear: 'The testicles are famous against the falling sickness,
concerning which affliction all children begotten at an
unclean season, on the eve of the Lord's-day, or any holy
day, are born epileptic, leprous or possessed.'

Another remedy for this illness involved snatching the
skin from a live snake, and just as the beaver, realizing why
men pursued it, castrated itself and threw its genitals down
before the hunters, so snakes were said to slough off their
own skins in order to escape with their lives.

Yet another means of obtaining relief from epilepsy was
to consume with bread the heart of a black jackass out of
doors on the first or second day of the moon, or to inhale
the odour of the afterbirth of an ass. A draught of human
blood, preferably that of a young man or gladiator, sucked
from a wound while he was still alive, was also considered
beneficial, and Galen, famous for his researches into anatomy in the second century A.D., recommended the skull of a
dead man, reduced to ashes and taken in drink. Pliny con-

demns the Greeks for using the leg-marrow and brains of
infants for this illness, and for detailing the flavour of the
various organs of the human body. He adds, 'To look at
human entrails is considered sin; what must it be to eat
them.'

Throughout the centuries under review mental disorders
were not well understood and sufferers were often very
harshly treated. They might be locked in darkened rooms,
starved, whipped and tormented. Bartholomew Anglicus
stresses the importance of urgent action in cases where the
symptoms include 'woodness,* and continual waking,
moving and casting about the eyes, raging, stretching, and
casting out of hands, moving and wagging of the head,
grinding and gnashing together of the teeth . . .' Such poor
souls, Bartholomew Anglicus counselled, should be starved
into sanity. Their nourishment had to be 'full, scarce, as
crumbs of bread, which must be many times wet in water'.
The treatment offered was to be as follows:

. . . in the beginning the patient's head be shaven, and
washed in lukewarm vinegar, and that he be well kept or
bound in a dark place. Diverse shapes of faces and sem-
blance of painting shall not be shewed tofore him, lest he be
tarred with woodness. All that be about him shall be com-
manded to be still and in silence; men shall not answer his
nice words. In the beginning of the medicine he shall be let
blood in a vein of the forehead, and bled as much as will fill
an egg-shell. Afore all things (if virtue and age suffereth) he
shall bleed in the head vein. Over all things, with ointment
and balming men shall labour to bring him asleep. The head
that is shaven shall be plastered with the lungs of a swine, or
of a wether, or of a sheep; the temples and forehead shall be
anointed with the juice of lettuce or of poppy. If after these
medicines are laid thus to, the woodness dureth three days
without sleep, there is no hope of recovery.

Clearly, nothing but sympathy prompted these horrendous
and complicated measures. A cure for 'dotage, head melancholy, and such diseases of the brain', recommended by
Burton, returns to the old principle of curing the sick
human being with the corresponding bits of a healthy

* madness.

animal, though it is not clear why the virginity of the beast is stressed here:

Take a ram's head that never meddled with an ewe, cutt off at a blow, and the horns only taken away, boil it well, skin and wool together; after it is well sod,* take out the brains, and put these spices to it . . . and heat them in a platter upon a chafing dish of coals together, stirring them well, that they do not burn; take heed it be not overmuch dried, or drier than a calf's brains ready to be eaten. Keep it so prepared, and for three days give it to the patient fasting. . . .

For all their shortcomings, these were genuine attempts to treat madness. Itinerant charlatans in medieval Europe, however, exploited the general ignorance about insanity to make large sums of money. They cut the patient's skull and pretended by sleight-of-hand to remove a stone from inside the head. After this piece of gross deception the sufferer was declared cured.

The Middle Ages had no monopoly in ill treating the mentally disturbed: from Bedlam in the sixteenth century to the nineteenth-century rector of Hauxwell in Yorkshire, who said of his incarceration in a repressive lunatic asylum, 'No time can blot it from my memory, were I to live till the day of doom'; and further to the inhumanities of our own day, this category of sick person has consistently suffered at the hands of the healthy. But even if we do not blame our ancestors for the head-shaving and starvation imposed on mental breakdown, we cannot help wondering if the patient ever survived the cure.

With such treatment in store (not to mention the probable fatal outcome), mankind had a special horror of the bites of rabid animals. Hydrophobia was apparently common. Burton, in his *Anatomy of Melancholy*, describes it as:

. . . a kind of madness, well known in every village, which comes by the biting of a mad dog, or scratching . . . so called because the parties affected cannot endure the sight of water, or any liquor, supposing they see a mad dog in it. And which is more wonderful, though they be very dry (as in this malady they are), they will rather die than drink.

* boiled.

Though some ancient writers were uncertain whether hydrophobia was a bodily illness or a mental one, Burton had no doubt of its exact nature:

The part affected is the brain: the cause, poison that comes from the mad dog, which is so hot and dry that it consumes all the moisture in the body. Hildesheim relates of some that died so mad; and being cut up, had no water, scarce blood, or any moisture left in them. To such as are so affected, the fear of water begins at fourteen days after they are bitten, to some again not till forty or sixty days after: commonly . . . they begin to rave, fly water and glasses, to look red and swell in the face, about twenty days after (if some remedy be not taken meantime) to lie awake, to be pensive, sad, to see strange visions, to bark and howl, to fall into a swoon, and oftentimes fits of the falling sickness. Some say, little things like whelps will be seen in their urines. If any of these signs appear, they are past recovery.

If the medical treatises are to be trusted, bites and stings of all sorts were an everyday hazard, and the demand for antidotes was steady. Very often animals provided the remedy for afflictions caused by animals. Snake bite, for example, could be treated with she-goat's water and vinegar, or, according to Aelian, with she-goat's dung boiled down in wine. As in so many remedies, it is not made clear whether the patient had to apply the concoction or swallow it.

Another particularly spectacular cure for snake-bite noted by Pliny was to swallow the testicles of a hippopotamus in water. Presumably few people would have been able to take advantage of this recipe since it must have been difficult to get hold of the main ingredient. For the dangerous bite of the hairy monkey-spider, said to cause trembling, chest pains, and stoppages of the bladder and bowel, Aelian recommends eating a river-crab.

If a man were unlucky enough to be stung by a scolopendra, the most formidable of centipedes, he could pour his own urine over his head as an antidote. Pliny even thought it necessary to include a remedy for those people who had been bitten by another human being, suggesting for this kind of mishap an application of boiled beef or veal.

As for the bites of dogs, mad or otherwise, these could be treated with an ointment made of axle-grease and lime, or by drinking a decoction of the dung of the badger, the cuckoo and the swallow.

Of special, and even obsessive, interest to mankind down the ages have been the beauty and sexual attractions of the individual, as well as the health of the various organs of the body associated with sex and with the procreation and birth of children. Classical and medieval medical treatises abound with cosmetic recipes and cures for facial imperfections. The woman who desired rosy cheeks, for instance, was advised by Pliny to rub them with bull's dung. Freckles were regarded as a serious blemish, and not only reduced sexual attractiveness but also debarred people from assisting at any form of magic ritual. A salve of billy-goat's gall with sulphur could, however, be applied in an effort to remove them.

Thinning hair was as much a problem to the Romans of the first century A.D. as it is to some men today, and to encourage a more luxuriant growth of hair whilst at the same time preventing greyness they were advised to swallow the genitals of an ass reduced to ashes. Those already afflicted with baldness could use bear's grease mixed with laudanum and adiantum. The growth of eyelashes could be stimulated by eating crow's brains, and sparse eyebrows could be improved with an application of lamp-black mixed with bear's grease. Alternatively they could be simply darkened by rubbing crushed flies into them.

Naturally the breath was considered important, and those who desired the 'ring of confidence' advertised by today's toothpaste manufacturers could rinse out the mouth with the ash of hare's head mixed with nard. If a man had a loose tooth, he was urged to tighten it with a mouthwash made from the ash of a deer's horn—a recipe less arbitrary than at first appears: horns and teeth were taken to be two, possibly alternative, manifestations of the same basic substance. As Bartholomew Anglicus explains: 'Also some beestis haue teeth in eyther Jowe and some haue only in the nether Jowe. And those whyche haue no teeth in the ouer Jowe ben hornyd/ for that matere passith and torneth in to hornes.'

The dung of the crocodile, said to possess an enchanting fragrance, was another aid to beauty, as the bestiarists pointed out: 'Its dung provides an ointment with which old and wrinkled whores anoint their figures and are made beautiful, until the flowing sweat of their efforts washes it away.' *

Remedies for genital disorders include applications of unsalted axle-grease for diseases of the male genitals and anus, or of cheese made from goat's milk, pounded down and liberally applied to carbuncles of the genital organs. Swollen testicles could be soothed by calf's dung boiled in vinegar, and sagging testicles made firm by applying the slime of snails.

These remedies were designed to cure physical ailments which were readily apparent. Nevertheless it was realized that even a normal, healthy person might find that desire was absent, or suffer from inhibitions which hindered sexual enjoyment. Others might wish to increase their existing sexual prowess by using some form of external stimulant.

For such people a wide range of aphrodisiacs was available. One could, for instance, take dried horse testicles, or the muzzle and feet of the scinos (a small lizard) in white wine seasoned with pepper, or the seminal fluid from a mare after copulation. Lizards drowned in a man's urine were powerful love philtres, though to the person who actually provided the urine they acted as an antaphrodisiac.

A man willing to risk death in order to enjoy his lust to the full could try snatching the teeth from a live crocodile to wear as an amulet. Topsell (1607) suggests a less hazardous means of improving a man's sexual capacity, presumably by ensuring a good erection, though the precise effect of the remedy is not actually specified: 'Marcellus saith, that the tooth of a horse being beaten and crushed into very small powder, and being sprinkled on a Man's genital does much profit and very effectually help him.'

Of course such preparations are useless if the object of

* T. H. White, p. 50.

lust rejects her would-be lover. But Pliny tells us that the
anus of a hyena worn by a man as an amulet on his left arm
renders him absolutely irresistible, so that he becomes
capable of seducing any woman desired. An even more
potent love-charm, capable of driving men and women
alike into a frenzy of desire, is recorded by Aelian:

When a mare gives birth, some say that a small piece of
flesh is attached to the foal's forehead, others say to its loin,
others again to its genitals. This piece the mare bites off and
destroys; and it is called 'Mare's-frenzy'. It is because
Nature has pity and compassion on horses that this occurs,
for (they say) had this continued to be attached always to the
foal, both horses and mares would be inflamed with a
passion for uncontrolled mating. Now those who tend
horses are fully aware of this and if they chance to need the
aforesaid piece of flesh with the design of kindling the fires
of Love in some person, they watch the Pregnant Mare, and
directly she bears the foal they seize it, cut off the piece of
flesh, and deposit it in a Mare's hoof, for there alone will it
be securely kept and stored away. As to the foal, they sacri-
fice it to the rising sun, for its dam refuses to suckle it any
more now that it has lost its birth token and no longer
possesses the premise of her affection. For it is by eating that
piece of flesh that the dam begins to love her offspring. But
any man who as a result of some plot tastes of that piece of
flesh becomes possessed and consumed by an incontinent
desire and cries aloud, and cannot be controlled from going
after even the ugliest boys and grown women of repellent
aspect. And he proclaims his affliction and tells those whom
he meets how he is being driven mad. And his body pines
and wastes away and his mind is agitated by erotic frenzy.

Yet even a woman who is basically willing might for
various reasons, such as recent childbirth or excessive
modesty, be unable to enjoy sexual intercourse. Again
Topsell comes to the rescue with a capital remedy:

The genital of a gelded Horse, dryed in an Oven, beaten
to powder, and given twice or thrice in a little hot broth to
drink unto the party so grieved, is by Pliny accounted an
excellent and approved remedy for the seconds* of a woman.
The foam of a Horse, or the dust of a Horse hoof dryed, is

* afterbirth.

very good to drive away shamefastness, being anointed with a certain titulation.

As to the frustrated woman who finds herself married to a homosexual, Pliny suggests that her husband should swallow a hyena's genitals in honey, and adds, 'nay the peace of the whole household is assured by keeping in the home these genitals and a vertebra [of the hyena] with the hide still adhering to them.'

Some people's requirements were exactly the opposite. There was a steady demand for antaphrodisiacs; from wives worn out by ceaseless childbearing who wished to dampen their husbands' ardour, and from men determined to keep their wives faithful. Moreover, antaphrodisiacs could be self-administered by people who, from religious scruples, or because they feared syphilis, or because they believed that it shortened life, wished to abstain from sexual intercourse.

According to Pliny, lynx nails and hide, reduced to ash, were a powerful antaphrodisiac: 'They say that these ashes, taken in drink by men check shameful conduct, and sprinkled on women lustful desire.'

For men, the application of mouse dung to the genital organs was equally successful. One can see why few women could have been willing to accept a man's attentions once he had daubed himself with such an offensive substance. Alternatives, suitable for either sex, were scinos' broth with honey, or the hide of the left side of the forehead of a hippopotamus worn as an amulet in the groin. Men who wished to avoid the horns of cuckoldry could massage their wives with an obnoxious potion or slip them a drink of thinly disguised urine, as an antaphrodisiac. Pliny gives an account of this: 'Osthanes says that if the loins of a woman are rubbed thoroughly with the blood of a tick from a black wild-bull, she will be disgusted with sexual intercourse, and also with her love if she drinks the urine of a he-goat, nard being added to disguise the foul taste.'

Just as there were some who wished to avoid sexual intercourse, so there were others who wished to enjoy it to the full but without the resulting pregnancy. On the whole, contraception was frowned on by the ancient writers, though some considered its use justified on medical grounds as, for instance, in the case of married women whose health was being impaired through too much child-bearing. It was only because of the urgent needs of such women that writers like Pliny found it within their conscience to recommend a contraceptive, as he explains in the following passage:

There is also a third kind of phalangium, a hairy spider with an enormous head. When this is cut open, there are said to be found inside two little worms, which, tied in a deer skin as an amulet on women before sunrise, act as a contraceptive. . . . They retain this property for a year. Of all such preventives this would only be right for me to mention, to help those women who are so prolific that they stand in need of such a respite.

It may seem remarkable that anyone could possibly have thought of adopting such a gruesome method of contraception, but the subject has to be looked at in the light of the exceptionally high mortality rate among women in childbirth. There is an element of risk involved in pregnancy and labour even today, but thanks to painstaking research, modern equipment and excellent medical services, that risk is now minimal. But throughout most of history the danger to life has been very serious, and existed whether it was the first pregnancy or the fourteenth.

The Caesarian operation has been widely known for many centuries, having been named after Julius Caesar, who was reputedly delivered by this method. This tends to give the impression of reasonably advanced techniques, yet in fact women rarely survived the operation, and it was usually performed only when the mother was already dead. Nothing at all could be done in such cases as a breech birth, for there were no obstetric instruments. In any event, there would have been nobody available to use them, for men were kept away from women in childbirth, and there were no female medical practitioners. Women in labour were not allowed into such hospitals as existed, for there were no anaesthetics to relieve their sufferings, and their screams would have disturbed other patients. Pregnant women could therefore look only to the midwife, who was of very little real help. In the light of these circumstances, it is hardly surprising that women were prepared to accept any form of contraceptive, however gruesome. Sadly, these methods were of course totally ineffectual. As if her problems were not already great enough, a woman's efforts to avoid conception could be frustrated if her husband put into practice an animal charm described by Pliny: 'Women unwilling to conceive are forced to do so by hairs from the tail of a she-mule, pulled out during the animal copulation and entwined during the human.'

Once pregnant, and keen to survive the experience, women placed their faith in any primitive remedy which was held to be beneficial. Among the animal substances recommended to them were the tongue of a chameleon, worn as an amulet to remove peril from labour, wolf's liver or powdered boar's dung taken in drink to ease birth pains, and the odours of fat from the loins of a hyena to secure an immediate delivery. Swallowing the liquid from a weasel's uterus discharged through its genitals was held to be very beneficial to women in labour.

Miscarriages, it was thought, could be avoided by wearing as an amulet the small stones swallowed by pregnant hinds and found in their excrement or uterus. Pliny recommends an alternative amulet: 'A woman is guaranteed never to miscarry if, tied round her neck in gazelle leather, she wears white flesh from a hyena's breast, seven hyena hairs, and the genital organ of a stag.'

On the other hand, there were some who, for various reasons, wished to procure an abortion. In such cases, the afterbirth of a bitch laid on the woman's loins would have the desired effect. Topsell gives another remedy:

There is yet moreover another excellent medicine proceeding from this dung [i.e. mouse dung], whereby the fruit in a woman's womb may be brought forth either dead or putrefied, without any hurt or prejudice unto the woman, which is thus; First to take Egyptian Salt, Mouse-dung, and Gourds which are sowen in Woods; and afterwards to pour in half a pinte of Hony, being half boyled, and to cast one dram of Rozen into the Hony, the Gourds and the Mousedung, and beat them well and thoroughly together, and then rowl them up, and fashion them in the manner of Acorns, and put them to the belly of the party so grieved, as often as you shall think it meet and convenient.

Inability to produce children struck directly at the sex-pride of the individual, a point at which people were, and still are, especially vulnerable. In cases of infertility it was usual to assume that the fault lay with the woman, and various remedies were recommended to deal with barrenness. These included anointing the uterus with calf's gall, or with a mixture of bull's gall, serpent's fat, copper rust and honey before sexual intercourse, or with goat's gall after menstruation. Pessaries made from the faeces of babies voided in the uterus were thought to be particularly beneficial. Five or more little earthworms swallowed in drink were also said to promote conception.

But if cures of this kind failed, infertility was often attributed to witchcraft practised by an enemy. Pliny tells us that eunuch's water would counteract the sorcery which prevents fertility, though he omits to say precisely how it should be used. However, those who were unable to obtain the services of an obliging eunuch could instead let their own morning urine run down over their feet.

An alternative, of course, was to try to find the witch who from malice had caused the barrenness. The Caroline lyrist Robert Herrick suggests how the witch can be located, once again by making use of urine:

> To house the hag, you must doe this,
> Commix with Meale a little Pisse
> Of him bewicht: then forthwith make
> A little wafer or a Cake;
> And this rawly bak't will bring
> The old Hag in. No surer thing.

Belief in witchcraft was very real, and by the middle of the seventeenth century had reached its climax in England. It was not confined to people of low intelligence but was firmly upheld by some of the most highly educated men

then living. Sir Thomas Browne, in his *Religio Medici*, makes
it clear that in his view those who do not believe in witches
must be atheists: 'For my part, I have ever believed, and
do now know, that there are Witches: they that doubt of
these, do not onely deny them, but Spirits; and are obliquely
and upon consequence a sort not of Infidels, but Atheists.'

King James the First, shortly before he succeeded to the
English throne, wrote a book called *Daemonologie*, first published in 1597, in which he both explains and denounces
withcraft as he understood it. He expresses his conviction
that witches have power over illness, being able to inflict
pain or disease on other people, or to cure them at will. In
particular he mentions their capacity for causing either
impotence or excessive sexuality:

Witches can, by the power of their Master [the Devil] cure
or cast on disseases: Now by these same reasones, that
proues their power by the Deuill of disseases in generall, is
as well proued their power in speciall: as of weaking the
nature of some men, to make them vnable for women: and
making it to abound in others, more then the ordinary
course of nature would permit.

Printed books about witchcraft from the fifteenth century
onwards, when witch-hunting with all its terrible conse-
quences was building up to a climax, and men and women
could be mercilessly tortured on no better evidence than
hearsay, laid particularly heavy emphasis on sex, for witches
were believed not only to interfere with the sex lives of
others but also to submit to sexual intercourse with devils.

Public demand for information on this latter point was
seemingly insatiable. One of the weighty problems with
which men were preoccupied was how the devil, being an
incorporeal spirit, could not only go through the motions
of coition but also ejaculate semen. Though some believed
that he did this by taking over dead bodies, the most
popular theory was that he obtained sperm from vigorous
men, either by stealing their nocturnal emissions or by
masquerading as a woman and receiving it during copulation, before reassuming male form in order to impregnate
the chosen witches.

When it came to animal remedies, there was really very little difference between many of the potions offered by doctors and those used by so-called witches. Pliny's recommendation to use lynx nails as an antaphrodisiac was not far removed from the use made by Anne Bodenham, one of many old women condemned to death for witchcraft in this country, of her own nail parings to induce drunkenness and madness:

... and the Witch gave her a powder, Dill leaves, and the paring of her own nails; all which the maid was to give to her Mistris; the powder was to be put in the Young Gentle-womens Mistress Sarah and Mistress Anne Goddards drink or broth, to rot their guts in their bellies; the leaves to rub about the brims of the pot, to make their teeth fall out of their heads; and the paring of the nails to make them drunk and mad.

A knowledge of magical recipes and ritual, either to bring good or ill, was part of every person's educational background, and would probably have been used by many, if the occasion demanded. Sir Kenelm Digby, for instance, in his *Late Discourse*, published in 1658, describes a method of causing pain by supernatural means as an act of revenge:

If it happens that there be a Farmer ... who keeps more neatly the approaches to his house than his neighbours do, the boyes use to come hither ... when it begins to be dark, to discharge their bellies there ... but they who are aquainted with this trick go presently and fire red-hot a broach or fire-shovel, and then thrust it into the excrements all hot, and heat it again oftentimes to the same purpose; In the mean-time the boy which made the ordure feels a kind of pain, and collick in his bowells, with an inflamation in his fundament.

This punishment could be avoided if the boy carried the pastern bone of a hare, but if successfully carried out it would seem more severe than the nature of the offence would warrant. In any event to most modern readers this would seem to be an act of witchcraft. Yet by strict defini-tion it was not so, for there was apparently no direct commerce with the devil. Sometimes, on the other hand, it was freely admitted that witches used their powers only to effect cures, but nevertheless this was not regarded as a valid excuse and could not save them from torture and death. For the real distinction between recognized medical practice and witchcraft lay in the supposed direct communion between witch and devil, either through invocation and ritual, or through sexual intercourse. So it happened that because of the absence of invocation, physicians could practise their arts with impunity, though the animal substances, etc., which they used were similar to the potions brewed by the witches in *Macbeth* from such ingredients as

> Scale of dragon, tooth of wolf;
> Witches' mummy; maw, and gulf
> Of the ravin'd salt-sea shark. . . .

This, then, was the general state of medical practice in the period covered by this book. By and large men were at the mercy of various types of medical practitioners, as Pliny explains:

Accordingly, heavens knows, the medical profession is the only one in which anybody professing to be a physician is at once trusted, although nowhere else is an untruth more dangerous. . . . Besides this, there is no law to punish criminal ignorance, no instance of retribution. Physicians acquire their knowledge from our dangers, making experiments at the cost of our lives. Only a physician can commit homicide with complete impunity.

Yet besides the witches, the itinerant charlatans, the monks and the barbers, who offered their unicorn horn and their gilded pellets of horse dung or testicles of the hippopotamus, were some doctors filled with a genuine desire to heal, and who rendered a valid service to their patients, offering the best treatment available in their own era. Bartholomew Anglicus describes this kind of doctor:

Then consider thou shortly hereof, that a physician visiteth oft the houses and countries of sick men. And seeketh and searcheth the causes and circumstances of the sicknesses, and arrayeth and bringeth with him divers and contrary medicines. And he refuseth not to grope and handle and to wipe and cleanse wounds of sick men. And he behooteth * to all men hope and trust of recovering of

* promises.

health; and saith that he will softly burn that which shall be burnt, and cut that which shall be cut. . . . A good leech leaveth not cutting or burning for weeping of the patient. And he hideth and covereth the bitterness of the medicine with some manner of sweetness. He drinketh and tasteth of the medicine, though it be bitter: that it be not against the sick man's heart, and refraineth the sick man of meat and drink; and letteth him have his own will, of the whose health is neither hope nor trust of recovering.

Bibliography

AELIANUS, CLAUDIUS, *De natura animalium*. Trans. A. F. Scholfield. Heinemann, London, 1958–60.

ALBERTUS MAGNUS, *De Animalibus*. Rome, 1478.

ALDROVANDUS, *Opera omnia*: de avibus; de quadrupedibus solidipedibus; de piscibus; de quadrupedibus digitatis; serpentum et draconum historiae. Frankfurt and Bonn, 1611–40.

ALLATIUS, LEO (or ALLACCI, LEONE), *S.P.N. Eustathii . . . in Hexahemeron commentarius:* ac de Engastrimytho dissertatio adversus Origenem. Lyon, 1629.

ALLEN, J. ROMILLY, *Christian Symbolism in Great Britain and Ireland before the Thirteenth Century*. London, 1887.
'On the Norman Doorway at Alne in Yorkshire'. *Journal of the British Archaeological Association*, vol. XLII, pp. 143–58.

ANET, CLAUDE, 'The Mana fi-i-Heiwan'. *Burlington Magazine*, vol. XXIII, pp. 224–31, 261, 6 plates. London, 1913.

ANON., *Delectable Demaundes and Pleasant Questions. . . .* London, 1566.

ANON., *The Dialogues of Creatures Moralysed*. London, c. 1535.

ANON., *The Myrrour and dyscrypcyon of the World*. London, 1527.

ARISTOTLE, *Generation of Animals*. Trans. A. L. Peck. Loeb Classical Library, Heinemann, London, 1943.
Historia Animalium. Trans. A. L. Peck. Loeb Classical Library, Heinemann, London, 1965.

BARBER, RICHARD, and RICHES, ANNE, *A Dictionary of Fabulous Beasts*. Macmillan, London, 1971.

BARTHOLOMAEUS ANGLICUS, *De Proprietatibus Rerum*. Cologne, c. 1372. English editions by Trevisa, London, 1495; Dr Stephen Batman, London, 1582.

BINYON, LAURENCE, *The Flight of the Dragon*. John Murray, London, 1911.

BISI, ANNA M., *Il Grifone*, storia di un motivo iconografico dell' antico oriente mediterranea. Rome, 1965.

BODENHEIMER, F. S. and RABINOWITZ, A., *Timotheus of Gaza on Animals*. Paris, Leiden, 1950.

BODIN, JEAN, *Universae naturae theatrum*. Lugduni, 1596.

BORGES, JORGE LUIS, and GUERRERO, M., *Manuel de zoologia fantastica*. Mexico, 1957.

BROWNE, SIR THOMAS, *Religio Medici*. London, 1643.

The Works of Sir Thomas Browne, ed. Geoffrey Keynes. Faber & Gwyer, London, 1928.

BURTON, ROBERT, *Anatomy of Melancholy*, 1621. Everyman's Library edition, J. M. Dent, London, 1961.

CAHIER, CHARLES, *Caractéristiques des Saints dans l'Art Populaire*. Paris, 1844.

CAHIER, CHARLES, and MARTIN, ARTHUR M., *Monographie de la Cathédrale de Bourges, ou Vitraux de Bourges*. Paris, 1841–4.

Mélanges d'Archéologie, 4 vols. Paris, 1847–58.

Suite aux Mélanges d'Archéologie. . . . Publiée par le survivant (C. Cahier), 2 vols. Paris, 1868.

CARLILL, JAMES, *Physiologus*. London, 1824.

CARLILL, JAMES, and STALLYBRASS, W. H. S. (eds.) *The Epic of the Beast*. London, 1924.

CARMODY, F. J., *Physiologus latinus*. Éditions préliminaires, versio B. Paris, 1939.

Physiologus Latinus versio v. University of California Publications in Classical Philology, vol. 12 no. 7. Berkeley, 1941.

Quotations in the Latin Physiologus from Latin Bibles earlier than the Vulgate. University of California Publications in Classical Philology, vol. 13 no. 1. Berkeley, 1944.

CARROLL, WILLIAM MEREDITH, *Animal Conventions in English, Renaissance Non-Religious Prose (1550–1600)*. New York, 1954.

CHAUCER, GEOFFREY, *The Parliament of Fowles*. Boston, 1877.

CHESTER, ROBERT, *Love's Martyr*. London, 1611.

COLLINS, ARTHUR H., *Symbolism of Animals and Birds Represented in English Church Architecture*. London, 1913.

COOK, ALBERT STANBURROUGH, and PITMAN, JAMES HALL, *The Old English Physiologus*. New Haven, 1921.

CTESIAS, *Ctesiae Cnidii Operum Reliquaiae*. Extracts of the *Indica* of Ctesias made by Photius, ninth-century Patriarch of Constantinople, ed. Baehr. Frankfurt, 1824.

DAHLERUP, VERNER, *Physiologus i to islandske bearbejdelser*. Copenhagen, 1889.

DARDANO, MAURIZIO, 'Note sul Bestiario toscano'. *L'Italia dialettale*, vol. 35, pp. 29–117. 1967.

DA VINCI, LEONARDO, *Frammenti Letterari e filosofici*. Florence, 1899.

DAVIS, J. I. (ed.), *Libellus de natura animalium*. William Dawson, London, 1958.

DE BEAUVAIS, VINCENT, *Bibliotheca mundi*, bks 16–20. Antwerp, 1624.

DEBIDOUR, V. H., *Le Bestiare sculpté du Moyen Âge en France*. Paris, 1961.

DE FOLIETO, HUGO, 'De Bestiis'. Reproduced in J. P. Migne, *Patrologia Latina*, CLXXVII, pp. 13–164, Paris, 1854, and attributed, probably falsely, to Hugo de Saint-Victoire.

DE FOURNIVAL, RICHARD, *Le Bestiare d'amour*, ed. C. Hippeau. Paris, 1860.

DE LILLE, ALAIN, 'De planctu naturae', *c.* 1160–70. Text in J. P. Migne, *Patrologia Latina*, CCX. Paris, 1866.

DE LOREY, E., 'Le bestiare de l'Escurial'. *The Art News*, June, 1935, New York.

DE SAINT-VICTOIRE, HUGO. *See* de Folieto.

DE VALDECEBRO, ANDRES FERRER, *Govierno general, moral y politico*. Madrid, 1683.

DRUCE, G. C., 'The Symbolism of the goat on the Norman font at Thames Ditton'. Reprinted from *Surrey Archaeological Collections*, vol. xxi. Roworth, London, 1908.
'The Sybill Arms at Little Mote, Eynsford'. Reprinted from *Archaeologia Cantiana*. Mitchell Hughes and Clarice. London, 1909.
'The Amphisbaena and its connexions in ecclesiastical art and architecture'. Reprinted from *The Archaeological Journal*, vol. lxvii, no. 268; 2nd series, vol. xvii, no. 4, pp. 285–317. Hunt, Barnard, London, 1910.
'The Symbolism of the crocodile in the Middle Ages'. Reprinted from *The Archaeological Journal*, vol. lxvi, no. 264; 2nd series, vol. xvi, no. 4, pp. 311–38. Hunt, Barnard, London, 1910.
'Notes on the history of the heraldic jall or yale'. Reprinted from *The Archaeological Journal*, vol. lxviii, no. 271; 2nd series, vol. xviii, no. 3, pp. 175–99. Hunt, Barnard, London, 1911.
'The Caladrius and its legend, sculptured upon the twelfth-century doorway of Alne Church, Yorkshire'. Reprinted from *The Archaeological Journal*, vol. lxix, no. 276; 2nd series, vol. xix, no. 4, pp. 381–416. Hunt, Barnard, London, 1913.
'Some abnormal and composite human forms in English church architecture'. Reprinted from *The Archaeological Journal*, vol. lxxii, no. 286; 2nd series, vol. xxii, no. 2, pp. 135–186. Royal Archaeological Institute, London, 1915.
'The Legend of the Serra or Saw-fish'. Extract from the *Proceedings of the Society of Antiquaries*, 1918, 2nd series, vol. xxxi, pp. 20–35. (No imprint given.)

'The Elephant in mediaeval legend and art'. Reprinted from *The Archaeological Journal*, vol. lxxvi, nos. 301–4; 2nd series, vol. xxvi, nos. 1–4, pp. 1–73, Royal Archaeological Institute, London, 1919.

'The Mediaeval bestiaries, and their influence on ecclesiastical decorative art'. Reprinted from the *Journal of the British Archaeological Association*, December. London, 1919.

'The Mediaeval bestiaries and their influence . . . II'. Reprinted from the *Journal of the British Archaeological Association*, December. London, 1920.

'An account of the Μυρμηκολέων or Ant-lion.' Reprinted from the *Antiquaries' Journal*, October, 1923, vol. iii, no. 4. Society of Antiquaries. London, 1923.

'The Pelican in the Black Prince's Chantry'. *Canterbury Cathedral Chronicle*, October, 1934, no. 19.

'The Bestiary of Guillaume Le Clerc', originally written 1210–11. Translated into English. Ashford, Kent, 1936.

'The Lion and cubs in the Cloisters'. *Canterbury Cathedral Chronicle*, April, 1936, no. 23.

'Queen Camel Church bosses on the chancel roof'. *Proceedings of the Somersetshire Archaeological and Natural History Society*, vol. lxxxiii. London, 1937.

EDWARDES, M., and SPENCE, L., *Dictionary of Non-Classical Mythology*. J. M. Dent, London, 1912.

Encyclopaedia Britannica, 11th ed.; article 'Physiologus'.

ETTINGHAUSEN, R., *The Unicorn*. Washington, 1952.

FRANTZE, WOLFGANG, *Historia Animalium Sacra*. Wittenberg, 1612.

FRAY LUIS DE URRETA, *Historia de los Grandes y Remotos Reynos de la Etiopia, Monarchia del Emperador Ilamado Preste Iuan*. Valencia, 1610.

GARVER, MILTON, 'Some supplementary Italian bestiary chapters'. *Romanic Review*, vol. ii, pp. 308–27. Lancaster, 1920.

GARVER, MILTON, and MCKENZIE, K. (eds.), 'Il Bestiario toscano secondo la lezione dei condici di Parigi e di Roma.' *Studi romanci*, no. 8. Rome, 1903.

GASELEE, SIR STEPHEN, *Natural Science in England at the End of the Twelfth Century*. London, 1936.

GESNER, KONRAD, *Historia Animalium*, 5 vols. Zürich, 1551–87.

GIRALDUS (DE BARRY) CAMBRENSIS, Archdeacon of St David's, *Topographia Hiberniae*. Frankfurt, 1602.

GOLDSMID, EDMUND, *Un-natural History*. Edinburgh, 1886.

GOLDSTAUB, MAX, and WENDRINER, RICHARD, *Ein Toxovenezianischer Bestiarius*. Halle, 1892.

GORDON, ROBERT KAY (trans.), *Anglo-Saxon Poetry*. J. M. Dent, Everyman's Library, London, 1926.

GUILLAUME, CLERC DE NORMANDIE, *Le Bestiare Divin*, ed. M. C. Hippeau. Caen, 1852.

HAINES, FRANCIS, *Appaloosa, the spotted horse in art and history*. Austin, Texas, 1962.

HARTHAN, JOHN P., 'Mediaeval Bestiaries.' *Geographical Magazine*, vol. xxii, pp. 182–90. London, 1919.

HERMANNSSON, HALLDOR (ed), 'The Icelandic Physiologus' (facsimile edition). *Islandica*, vol. 27. Ithaca, New York, 1938.

HERODOTUS, *History*. Trans. George Rawlinson. Dent, Everyman's Library, London, 1910.

HEUVELMANS, BERNARD, *In the Wake of the Sea-Serpents*. Hart-Davis, London, 1968.

HILDEGARDE, ABBESS, *Physica*. Argentorati, 1533.

HOLMBERG, JOHN, *Eine mittelnieder Frankische Übertragung des Bestiare d'Amour*. Uppsala, 1925.

HORAPOLLO NILUS, *The Hieroglyphics*. Trans. A. T. Cory. London, 1840.

HUBER, A., *Der Abtissin St. Hildegardis myst. Tier-und-Artzeneyen-Buch*. Vienna, 1923.

INGUANEX, REV. DON MAURO, 'L'Esamerone di St. Ambrogio ridotto in versi da Alessandro monaco di M. Cassino.' *Rivista Storica Benedettina*, 1913.

ISIDORE OF SEVILLE, *Etymologae*. Strasbourg, ?1470.

IVES, SAMUEL A., and LEHMANN-HAUPT, HELLMUT, *An English Thirteenth-Century Bestiary*. New York, 1942.

JACKSON, BLOMFIELD, *Translation of the Hexameron*, in *A Select Library of the Nicene and Post-Nicene Fathers of the Christian Church*, vol. viii. Oxford, 1895.

JAMES, MONTAGUE RHODES, *The Peterborough Psalter and Bestiary*. Roxburgh Club, Oxford, 1921.
The Bestiary. Roxburgh Club, Oxford, 1928.

JANSON, H. W., *Apes and Ape Lore in the Middle Ages and Renaissance*. Warburg Institute, London, 1952.

KEMP-WELCH, ALICE, 'Beast Imagery and the Bestiary.' *Nineteenth Century and After*, vol. 54, pp. 501–9. London, 1903.

KLINGENDER, FRANCIS, *Animals in Art and Thought to the end of the Middle Ages*. Routledge and Kegan Paul, London, 1971.

KONSTANTINOVA, A., *Ein englisches Bestiar des zwölften Jahrhunderts in der Staatsbibliothek zu Leningrad*. Berlin, 1929.

KRAUS, FRANZ ZAVIER, *Kunst und Alterthum in Unter-Elsass*. Strasbourg, 1876.

KUHNS, LEVI OSCAR, *Bestiaries and Lapidaries*. With selections translated. Warner's Library of the World's Best Literature, vol. 4. 1860.

LAND, J. P. N., *Anecdota Syriaca*. Leiden, 1874.

LAUCHERT, FRIEDRICH, *Geschichte des Physiologus*. Strasbourg, 1889.

LEGH, GERARD, *The Accedens of Armorie*. London, 1562.

LEGRAND, EMILE (ed.), *Physiologus*. Paris, 1873.

LEHMANN-HAUPT, HELLMUT. *See* Ives, Samuel.

LUM, PETER, *Fabulous Beasts*. Thames and Hudson, London, 1952.

LYLY, JOHN, *Complete Works of John Lyly*, ed. R. Warwick Bond. Clarendon Press, Oxford, 1902.

MCCULLOCH, FLORENCE, 'The Waldensian bestiary and the *Libellus de Natura Animalium*'. *Medievalia et Humanistica*. Chapel Hill, USA, 1963.
'The Metamorphoses of the Asp in Latin and French Bestiaries'. *Studies in Philology*, I, vi. Chapel Hill, USA, 1959.
Mediaeval Latin and French Bestiaries. Chapel Hill, USA, 1960.

MCKENZIE, KENNETH, 'Unpublished Manuscripts of Italian Bestiaries.' *Modern Language Association Publication*, vol. 20, pp. 380–430. Cambridge, 1905. *See* also Garver and McKenzie.

MANDEVILLE, SIR JOHN, *The Bodley Version of Mandeville's Travels*, ed. M. C. Seymour. O.U.P. for Early English Text Society, London, 1963.

MANN, M. F., *Der Physiologus des Philipp von Thaün und seine Quellen*. Halle, 1884.
'Der Bestiare Divin des Guillaume le Clerc'. *Franzoesische Studien*, vol. 6, no. 2. Berlin, 1881.

MAPLET, JOHN, *The Diall of Destiny*. London, 1581.
A Greene Forest or a Naturall History . . . London, 1567.

MARSON, JOHN, 'The English Cistercians and the Bestiary'. *John Rylands Library Bulletin* vol. 39, pp. 146–70. Manchester, 1956.

MERES, FRANCIS, *Palladis Tamia*. London, 1598.

MILLAR, E. G., *A Thirteenth Century Bestiary in the Library of Alnwick Castle*. Roxburgh Club, Oxford, 1958.

MÖLLER, L. L., *Bestiarium Tiere und Kunst der letzteren fünf Jahrtausende*. Hamburg, 1962.

MØLLER-CHRISTENSEN, V., and JØRGENSEN, K. E. JORDT, *Encyclopedia of Bible Creatures*. Philadelphia, 1965.

MORRIS, R., *An Old English Miscellany*. London, 1872.

MULLER, SOPHUS, *Die Thierornamentik im Norden*. Hamburg, 1881.

MURDOCH, FLORENCE, *Trailing the Bestiaries*. Washington, 1932.

NAPIER, ARTHUR S. (ed.), *History of the Holy Rood-Tree, a Twelfth-Century Version of the Cross Legend*. London, 1894.

NECKAM, ALEXANDER, *De Naturis rerum*. London, 1858.

NICANDER, *The Poems and Poetical Fragments*, ed. and trans. A. S. F. Gow and A. F. Scholfield. Cambridge, Mass., 1953.

NORMAN, HENRY W., *The Anglo Saxon Version of the Hexameron of St. Basil, or, Be Godes Six Daga Weorcum*. London, 1848.

OGLU, MEHEMET AAGA, *A Note on the Manuscript of Manafi-al Hayawan*. New York, 1933.

OLAUS MAGNUS, *Historia de Gentibus Septentrionalibus*, Rome, 1555.

OPPIAN, *Cynegetica*. Lipsaie, 1813.
Vita Oppiani L. Lippii Collensis. Colle, 1478.

OUDEMANS, A. C., *The Great Sea-Serpent*. Leiden, 1892.

OVIDIUS NASO, PUBLIUS, *The Metamorphoses of Ovid*. Trans. William Caxton. London, 1480.

PEERS, ALISON, *The Book of Beasts*, trans. from the Catalon. London, 1927.

PETERS, E., *Der griechische Physiologus und seine orientalischen Übersetzungen*. Berlin, 1898.

PINDER, ULRICH, *Der beschlossen gart des rosenkrantz Marie*. Nuremberg, 1505.

PLINIUS SECUNDUS, CAIUS, *Natural History*, ed. H. Rackham. Loeb Classical Library, Heinemann, London, 1938.

RANDALL, RICHARD H., *A Cloisters Bestiary*. New York, 1960.

RENDELL, A. W., *Bishop Theobald: his metrical Physiologus*. J. and E. Bumpus, London, 1928.

ROBIN, P. ANSELL, *Animal Lore in English Literature*. John Murray, London, 1932.

RORIMER, JAMES J., *The Unicorn Tapestries at the Cloisters*. New York, 1962.

ST AMBROSE, *Hexameron*. Augsburg, 1472.

SALUSTE DU BARTAS, GUILLAUME DE, trans. Joshua Sylvester, *Du Bartas His Divine Weeks and Works*. London, 1592–1602.

SBORDONE, F., *Physiologus*. Mediolani, Italy, 1936.
Ricerche sulle funti e sulla composizione del Physiologus greco. Naples, 1936.

SEGRE, CESARE (ed.), *Li bestiaries d'amours di maistre Richart de Fournival e li response du bestiare*. Milan, 1957.

SELMER, CARL (ed.), *Navigatio Sancti Brendani Abbatis*. University of Notre Dame, 1959.

SERAPION THE YOUNGER, *El libro agregá de Serapion*. Venice, 1962.

SHEPHARD, ODELL, *The Lore of the Unicorn*. Houghton Mifflin, London, 1930.

SOLINUS, CAIUS JULIUS, *Polyhistor*. Coloniae, 1520.

STEWART, DESMOND, 'A Persian Bestiary'. *Early Islam*. New York, 1967.

STRZYGOWSKY, JOSEF, *Der Bilderkreis des griechischen Physiologus, Nach Handschriften der Bibliothek zu Smyrna bearbeitet*. Leipzig, 1899.

SWAN, JOHN, *Speculum Mundi*. Cambridge, 1635.

THAUN, PHILIPPE DE, *Le Bestiare de Philippe du Thaün*. Texte critique, publié avec introduction, notes et glossaire par

Emmanuel Walberg. Lund, 1900. *Li Livre des Creatures.*
Popular Treatises on Science, ed. T. Wright. London, 1841.

THEOBALDUS, EPISCOPUS, *Physiologus.* Cologne, 1497. *See* Rendell,
A. W.

THOMPSON, SIR D'ARCY WENTWORTH, *A Glossary of Greek Birds.*
Oxford, 1895.
Aristotle as a Biologist. Oxford, 1913.

TOPSELL, E., *The Historie of Foure-footed Beastes.* London, 1607.
*The Historie of Serpents, or The second Booke of living Creatures,
etc.* London, 1608.
*The History of Four-footed Beasts and Serpents . . . Whereunto is
now added, the Theater of Insects . . . by T. Muffet.* London, 1658.

TREVER, C., *The Dog Bird* (pamphlet). Leningrad, Hermitage, 1938.

TREVISA. *See* Bartholomew Anglicus.

TSYCHEN, O. G., *Physiologus Syrus.* Rostock, 1795.

VALENTINI, *Natur- und Materialienkammer aus Ost-Indianische Send-
Schreiben und Rapporten.* Frankfurt, 1704.

VIERT, PETER, *The Schoole of Beastes,* trans. I. B. London, 1585.

VILLETTE, CLAUDE, *Raisons de l'Office.* Paris, 1601.

VINYCOMBE, JOHN, *Fictitious and Symbolic Creatures in Art.* Chap-
man and Hall, London, 1906.

VIOLLET-LE-DUC, E. E., *Dictionnaire Raisonné de l'Architecture
Française du 11me au 16me Siècle.* Paris, 1853.

VIRGIL MARO, PUBLIUS, *The Georgics of Virgil,* trans. C. Day Lewis.
Jonathan Cape, London, 1940.

VON STEIGER, CHRISTOPH, and HOMBURGER, OTTO, *Physiologus
Bernensis.* Basle, 1964.

WATKINS, M. G., *Gleanings from the Natural History of the Ancients.*
London, 1896.

WELLMANN, M., 'Der Physiologus'. *Philologus,* supplement xxii.
Leipzig, 1931.

WHITE, B., 'Medieval Animal Lore', *Anglia,* vol. lxxii. 1954.

WHITE, T. H., *The Book of Beasts.* Jonathan Cape, London, 1954.

WRIGHT, THOMAS, *Popular Treatises on Science during the Middle Ages.*
London, 1841.
History of Caricature and the Grotesque. London, 1875.

WRIGHT, THOMAS, and HALLIWELL, J. O., *Reliquae Antiquae.*
London, 1841–3.

YOHANNAN, A., 'A manuscript of the Manafi'al-Haiawan in the
library of J. P. Morgan'. *Journal of American Oriental Society,*
vol. xxxvi, pp. 381–9, 1917.

Index